THE LITTLE PRINCE
PUTS ON HIS TIE

BORJA VILASECA

*A tale of personal growth
for getting back in touch with what really matters.*

Translated by Toni Crabb

INDEX

Explanatory note.

Prologue. This is not a job for cynics.

I.   Tell me how you lead and I'll tell you who you are.

II.   Some bosses are bad for your health.

III.   Modern slavery.

IV.   Suffering will get you nowhere.

V.   The true sceptic explores the unknown.

      Honesty, humility and courage.

      What is self-knowledge and what is its purpose?

      Is self-knowledge selfish behaviour?

      Reactivity is slavery.

      Consciously training to be proactive.

      Reality and the way you interpret it.

      The tyranny of egocentricity.

      The power of acceptance.

      The function of existential crises.

      What exactly changes when you change?

VI.   The pathology of success.

VII. Learning is the path and the aim.

      Taking responsibility.

      Anger, fear and sadness.

      What is the ego, how does it work, and what is its function?

      The difference between innocence, ignorance and wisdom.

      Happiness and inner peace go together.

      Questioning your belief system.

      Daring to give yourself what you need emotionally.

      The importance of cultivating your vital energy.

      The art of compassion.

VIII. In search of yourself.

IX. Careful! Power isolates and corrupts.
X. Maturity comes with realising you're not a victim of your circumstances.

Epilogue. If you really want to change the world, begin with yourself.
Thanks.

To my dad, and others who, like him, encourage and help their children to find their own way in life.

"The whole world steps aside for the man who knows where he is going."
ANTOINE DE SAINT-EXUPÉRY

EXPLANATORY NOTE

This book is not a novel. The story it tells is based on real people and events. It is, however, varnished with a thin layer of imagination in order to respect the anonymity of those in it. This was the only thing asked of me by the people behind the characters, all of them worthy of my deepest praise and acknowledgement.

This work was conceived just under three years ago. I was asked by my boss to write an article on a consulting firm employing seventy-three people which had experienced spectacular growth over the previous five years. The company had been running for nearly twenty years when, in 2002, management introduced a series of changes that led its total revenue to multiply one hundred and ten times, to a figure of $25 million in 2007.

As a journalist, I had specialised in organisational philosophy and psychology. I wrote about human beings, not normally about money, and tried to encourage other people to express their creativity and potential by giving readers access to the expert knowledge they needed. So it was hard for me to imagine why I should have been chosen to cover this particular story. But very soon after my interview with the company's boss – who'd recently been named Executive of the Year – I understood why.

The top executive, whom we'll call Ian Insley, was wearing a suit and tie just like any other; but there was something different about him. He spoke about his work with a contagious passion. To this day I can't remember having such an enthralling business conversation with anyone. We spoke of things such as the importance of self-knowledge, personal development and emotional intelligence, and the need to build a conscientious corporate culture which would merge companies' legitimate need for profit with the well-being of their workers, suppliers, customers, and the environment we all inhabit.

We even agreed on the fact that the materialistic mindset and individualistic, mercantile values upheld by capitalism are in decline. Insley felt that "Businesses are like human beings: they have needs, dreams and feelings," and so "They need to learn to become efficient, to grow sustainably and contribute something to the world around them." Thus, "The biggest challenge is to get each worker to believe in and enjoy his or her job, because it's the only way to give the life of a company a deeper meaning."

Just before we said goodbye, the interesting man shook my hand hard and whispered, "It's taken me a long time, but I've finally realised that the truly important things in life aren't visible to the naked eye. Only the heart can feel them."

My interview with Insley gave me an unexpected gift: the knowledge that genuineness and inspiration can be found everywhere, even in the top echelons of business. When I left his office after a two and a half hour talk, I was brimming with happiness and enthusiasm, and longing to know the ins and outs of the firm's amazing story.

The interview was followed by a period of research during which I followed the stories of each and every one of the people who'd contributed to the firm's success. In the process, I met its founder and chairman, now retired, and since then a good friend of mine, whom I will call George Lovejoy. After several visits to George's home, I finally found the revelation I was looking for. Apparently, the true turning point for the firm had come just a year before Ian Insley had taken over as general manager. In George's words, "What we are and what we have done is all due to the influence of another man, definitely the most extraordinary one I've ever met. You'll never see his face in the papers, but he's the one who's really behind it all. All the rest of us, including Ian, and myself of course, just played a supporting role."

This book aims to explain the events that led our anonymous hero to do what he did. And to emphasise the deep changes that human beings, and with them, the organisations they belong to, can go through once they become aware of their real potential, putting it to the service of a necessary, creative, sustainable, meaningful function. Although it might seem like I've written a novel, in actual fact, I insist, this book is the result of a fascinating, very thorough news report. At the request of George Lovejoy, the founder and chairman of the consulting firm, the prologue and epilogue are written by him. He and I have in common a mutual love of writing.

THE JOURNALIST.
6th April 2010.

PROLOGUE

THIS IS NOT A JOB FOR CYNICS

Living and being alive might seem like the same thing, but there's actually a vast difference between them. I had to die in order to understand that. Four minutes, thirty-seven seconds. That was exactly how long I was 'clinically dead', as the doctor in charge of the medical team who brought me back to life was later to tell me. I was forty-seven at the time, and had learnt very little of any worth about either myself or my life.

But I can happily say that that year, my life began again, with a triple bypass that woke me up from a deep sleep.

Seven years have gone by since I was resuscitated. So I'm officially in the seventh anniversary of the day my life began. I have a bit of a paunch, it's true, and prostrate problems, backache and wrinkles. But I really feel much younger than many of the thirty-year-olds I know. I'm not joking, I promise. Even my wife says I'm quite a stud now!

As far as I know, I haven't gone mad. Actually, I've never felt so sane. But what I'm about to tell is beyond all reason or logic. And it's hard, if not impossible, to scientifically prove. The most interesting account of it I've read is by two experts, a Swiss American doctor, Elizabeth Kübler-Ross, and an American professor, Kenneth Ring. They did a lot of research on what happens to people when they come face to face with death. Mostly, they concluded, those who survive reconnect with the wonder and magic of being alive, and start truly living.

I know this is hard to believe, and that many people won't, except for those who've been through the same thing. But I don't mind. I know who I am now. I've spent too many years trying to fit into society's expectations. And after wearing a mask for so long, I ended up forgetting who I'd been before I started wearing it. But by cultivating my self esteem, I've been rediscovering myself. I'm starting to know what it means to be yourself. I'm not a slave to others' opinions any more. I've freed myself of my obsession with being liked by other people, of the need to give them reasons to approve of me. My own conscience is my only judge now.

My near-death experience was a journey beyond this world. It must sound like a cliché, but I saw the light. I was enlightened! I'm not a Buddhist, or even religious. At the time I was a non-practising Catholic; or shall I say, an apathetic agnostic with little desire to think about anything I couldn't see with my eyes or touch with my hands.

Existentially speaking, I was so lazy I never bothered to question my social or cultural conditioning. I simply believed everything I'd been told in my childhood, living like a sheep who didn't even need a shepherd. I'm not afraid to admit that I followed the flock out of insecurity, comfort and inertia. I was a coward pretending to be a winner. Only now do I realise that I was choosing to fool myself rather than face my fears, emptiness and insecurity.

The only god I adored was money, I admit it. Year after year, I prayed for better and bigger purchases. Like a hamster on a wheel, I produced, consumed and evaded my dissatisfaction with reality. I sought for short-reaching pleasures so I wouldn't have to face the pain I'd accumulated over my lifetime. And the funniest thing of all is that I thought of my obsessive narcosis as 'fun'. The saddest thing, though, is that so much refusal to look inwards made me lose sight of myself.

Time has certainly given me the chance to see things more objectively, from a distance. I still don't understand how I could have been so naïve. I really thought satisfying my desires would lead to happiness. And not only did I believe it, but I made it my way of life! All I cared about was myself and my family. And even that's not entirely true – I hardly spent any time with my wife or three children. They've never been starved for anything material, but I see now that in love and affection they were living below the poverty line. Sometimes, when I feel vulnerable and show them my love, I still ask them to forgive me for having been absent from them for so many years. And I feel amazed every time they hug me and tell me it doesn't matter any more, and that the most important thing is the fact that I'm with them now.

But let's get back to my near-death experience; I'll talk about the rest later on. As I lay on the bed in the Intensive Care Unit, completely unconscious, for the first time in my life I felt something akin to peace, well-being and plenitude. In that calm, quiet state I felt separated from my body. I detached from it to observe myself from several metres above. With my own eyes, I watched the doctors and nurses struggling to keep me alive. They seemed more interested than I was in doing so.

And that was when a strange tunnel-like darkness came over me. My apologies to the sceptics, but yes, I saw a tenuously shining light in the distance. It was whitish with gold hues. As I got closer to it a feeling of love welled up in me. And here's another cliché: my whole life passed before me. It was a selection of the most representative moments in it. Not the best, but the most important ones. In actual fact, I remembered the most difficult experiences, the ones which had made me suffer the most. And I realised I hadn't appreciated them as I should have. In my regression I realised these moments had a very special function: they were there to make me develop and grow as a human being.

Just after that I heard a strange, faraway voice whispering to me.

"Trust in what you can't see and you'll begin to feel it... Commit yourself to what you feel and you'll really see it."

I don't know how long I was in that trance. But when I came back to my body, my pain also returned, and with it, clarity and comprehension. Days later my wife said in amazement that when I came out of my coma my eyes were shining in a special way. It was as if I'd been reborn. Wow! I'd been born again! And I've been a different person ever since.

As soon as I opened my eyes, I knew that my life's work hadn't even begun yet. I was fully conscious of everything I'd never been and everything I could still become; of what I hadn't done and could still do. The nurses watched as I cried like a baby. And my tears finally dissolved the invisible bandage over my eyes: I'd always demanded things of the people around me, and at work, but I never gave anything; I loved, but not with my heart. And so I felt dissatisfied, empty and alone.

When I came back to life I realised my life had a specific purpose. My heart beat, my blood was running through my brain, and three questions came to me insistently: Who am I? What can I do well? How can my life make other people happy? I didn't yet know how to answer them, but I gave thanks for having been given a second chance to find out, and to be coherent with what I discovered. And I was excited! I wanted to play like a kid again. But this time I'd play the game responsibly and conscientiously. This, at least for me, is the meaning of true maturity.

Many people think that this awakening of consciousness is a dream, a fantasy or a mere illusion. And I understand why. I'm sceptical too; I don't believe anything. The only thing that's changed in me is that I've become more open, and I recognise in all humility that the only things we can understand are the ones we've experienced. Also, the arrogance of thinking we know it all stops us from growing and developing. I don't want to play with words here; but all I know is that I know nothing. I've become an eternal apprentice. There's no better school than life. And no better training than learning to live.

The only thing I feel sure of is that the experience of nearly dying was the most life-changing thing that has ever happened to me. And I want to share it with anyone who will read it with an open mind, shedding their prejudices and limitations. Being reborn cured me of the disease known as cynicism. I'm no longer so demanding; I know how to give. And I don't waste my time trying to be loved. My desire is to love. Today, on my seventh birthday, I can say I feel fully human. That, I know, is my greatest victory. To quote Rabindranath Tagore, I've finally come to terms with the fact that "Only a life lived for others is a life worthwhile."

THE CHAIRMAN
8th August 2009

I
TELL ME HOW YOU LEAD
AND I'LL TELL YOU WHO YOU ARE

Monday 30th September 2002

Paul laughed out loud to himself. He'd been standing in front of the mirror for a quarter of an hour now and he felt that was enough. He wasn't a vain guy, though; he just didn't know how to do up his tie. Carefully, he folded it up and put it in his pocket. It was red, and he didn't have any others.

"Today could be a great day," he smiled, staring at himself. It didn't matter what kind of mood he woke up in. Every morning he said the same to himself. It was one of his daily rituals.

Before he left the house he opened the balcony door from his bedroom onto the small balcony, where his his silent flatmate lived.

"Here's breakfast," he whispered to her.

And as he watered the only rose on the bush, he added, "You're looking gorgeous."

He jumped on his bike and rode off to the headquarters of SAT, a consulting firm in advanced technological systems. Getting off, he smoothed down his jacket, rearranged his scarf and strode over to the doorway.

"Morning. Having a good day?"

"Do you want me to say 'fine', or really tell you how it's going?" grunted the old concierge in his smart suit.

"No need for formalities with me - I could be your son."

"And I could be your father. So you ought to show some respect," snapped the concierge.

"You're right. I'm sorry, I didn't mean to offend you."

The man took a deep breath. Finally, his expression relaxed. "I'll think about whether to forgive you," he muttered half-jokingly. He scratched his chin. "I'll decide whether I will or not once your work interview is over."

"How do you know...?"

"Well, there's been a sort of shark parade going through this entrance hall all morning - all of them dressed exactly the same, and walking really fast as if the world was about to end. And they all have that haughty look about them... vain as hell." His voice rose as he spoke. "Bunch of bad-mannered louts!" he added angrily. "What would it take for them to say a simple 'good morning'?"

Paul burst out laughing. The concierge didn't take too well to it. He was one of those people who like their unhappiness to be taken seriously. The man paused, then breathed in and tried to calm down.

"Anyway," he said, "something tells me you're different." Paul smiled.

"You're the only one who doesn't wear a tie." And, he thought to himself, the only one who bothered to say hello.

"Speaking of ties... What's your name, by the way?"

"Me? Bernard Martin," the man answered reluctantly. Paul shook his hand and introduced himself.

"Pleased to meet you, Bernard. I wonder, could I ask you a favour?"

"Me? Um..." he hesitated, trying hard not to show his curiosity.

"Would you be so kind as to show me how to do up this tie?"

The concierge chuckled. His sense of humour was kind of rusty, but it came to life.

"Yeah, why not! Come here, will you? You know something? You're a bit late, but I'm an old dog here - and I reckon you're going to get the job."

Just as Bernard Martin had said, the reception at SAT was full of black and grey suits and ties. It was a small room, but everyone in it was waiting silently. Nobody was talking to anyone else, but the look in their eyes said it all: all of them were after a single job.

"Look, could you please stop shouting?" said the gorgeous young receptionist as Paul stationed himself at her desk, smiling. "Ugh! Why do I sometimes have to be so rude!" she asked, looking at Paul and pointing at the phone. "I've told him three times that Mr. Lovejoy has been interviewing candidates the whole morning! I know it's urgent, but there's nothing I can do – he'll just have to wait for him to call back..."

She nodded at least ten times more into the mouthpiece, and finally brought the conversation to an end. "Yes, yes, yes, as you wish! Thank you so much for your patience. Goodbye." She hung up and pulled off her earpiece. "I can't stand it when they shout!" she exclaimed. "Some people are just too much. Christ, what a morning!"

Paul gently tried to meet her eyes. "I totally understand you," he said with a wink. "Man, my old boss was a shouter. He really brought out the worst in people. It wasn't words that came out of his mouth, but poison – we used to call him Mr. Cyanide."

They giggled mischievously together. "Oh, so you know what it's like," said the receptionist flirtatiously. She was a little more relaxed. "Why do people have to be so rude?"

"Maybe they just don't know how to act different," Paul replied. "I haven't met anyone yet who *enjoys* being rude."

He told her his name and stood chatting to her. Her name was Linda Orizio. Her bad mood vanished as they talked, and soon she was telling him about the interview he was about to have. Apparently the person due to conduct the interviews was the chief consultant, Ian Insley. But he hadn't been seen in the office for two weeks now. It was the first time in thirteen years he'd missed more than two days work.

"No-one knows why..." said Linda. "Knowing him, something really bad must have happened. Some people say he's off work for depression. That's why the chairman, Mr. Lovejoy, is personally interviewing the candidates."

Paul listened carefully, nodding encouragingly.

"Don't tell anyone this, but Mr. Lovejoy recently had a triple bypass. He nearly died! And ever since he came out we've all noticed he's acting weird. Really, really weird..."

Mr. Lovejoy' office door swung open, and Linda sat up straight and acted like she'd been talking about nothing in particular. The latest interviewee left the office with his head bowed, and the phone rang again. It was the chairman.

"I think we've found someone, Mr. Lovejoy," said Linda sweetly. She gave a couple of nods and then said, "Alright, I'll send him through."

To the consternation of the other interviewees, Paul walked straight through to the office.

He sat down in front of George Lovejoy, who looked him over, scratching his bald patch as he did so.

"Mr. Prince, I don't know if you realised, but you made a very good impression on our charming receptionist Linda," said the chairman.

"Call me Paul, please. Mr. Prince is my father."

A brief smile appeared at the corner of Mr. Lovejoy' mouth, but he corrected it straight away.

"Very well. Anyway, I mentioned Linda because she has a knack for spotting talented people... Actually, for the last three and a half hours I've been listening to people who are really good at talking, but know exactly how to say nothing at all. That's about twenty-five job candidates. And in that chair, right where you're sitting, I've seen ambition, greed, vanity, arrogance... they're like versions of myself when I was young, really. I'm telling you this because I just don't find all those common virtues so interesting," he said with a touch of sarcasm. "Right now I'm looking for something different. I want real talent. I want genuineness. Is that really too much to ask, I wonder?" he asked, looking up at the ceiling.

Then, he picked up what seemed to be Paul's CV and went on.

"So – it says here you're thirty years old, and you worked in the human resources department of a large consulting firm..." He went on.

"...Wait a minute," he said. "You haven't set foot in an office for the last three years? Is that true?"

"Yes. Also, I share my flat with a rose; my best friends are my books, and my favourite hobby is stargazing," George answered with a disarming smile.

Lovejoy gave a puzzled frown and cleared his throat.

"A rose?"

"Yes. She's beautiful." He felt around in his jacket pocket. "I think I have a photo here..."

The chairman scratched his nose, though it wasn't itching. He took a deep, nervous breath. In a hard voice, he answered, "No, don't. All roses look the same..."

"Or different. It depends on how you see them."

"Look – I'm not going to waste my time discussing roses here." Lovejoy lent back in his chair and resumed the interview in a more distant tone of voice.

"Could you tell me what exactly you've been up to over the past three years?"

"I went travelling."

"Travelling?"

"Yes, I travelled the world. I worked at whatever I could to pay for it as I went along."

"What made you decide to give up everything and head off?"

"It was easy. I was very unhappy when I worked at the consulting firm because I didn't know who I was or what I wanted to do with my life. I had nothing to lose, so I went travelling to find out. And it worked. That's why I'm here, now, sitting in front of you. This is exactly where I want to be. And the job is exactly the one I want to do. And seeing as you're allowing me to be so frank: I don't believe in coincidence, I believe things happen for a reason. I got back from Madagascar less than a month ago, and the day before yesterday I bought the newspaper for the first time – and as soon as I saw this job offer I knew it was the one I was searching for."

"Interesting," said the chairman. "Madagascar sounds like a faraway, poor, underdeveloped place. Am I wrong?"

"That depends on what you mean by development. I think we have a lot to learn from the people there. They're still in touch with nature, and they find it hard to understand how someone with a roof over their head and enough food to eat could feel depressed."

George Lovejoy thought of the chief consultat, Ian Insley.

"Well." He gave a smile, and then glanced back at Paul's CV. "Let's go on to something else, shall we? I see you're the only interviewee without an MBA – what do you have to say about that?"

"MBAs are very expensive. And what I want to learn can't be taught at business school, anyway."

"What kind of things do you want to learn?"

Paul had no need to hesitate. "How to know myself better so I can be happy and help others by doing a job that will generate real wealth for society."

Lovejoy stared at him, took a deep breath, and answered, "If what it says here is true, then you must have learnt that while you travelled... Please don't be offended by what I say; but this is the first time I've interviewed someone who places such a high value on the educational value of his own experience."

Rubbing his bald patch, he laid the CV on his desk and went on. "Paul, to tell you the truth, some years ago I wouldn't have even bothered to go on with this interview. I probably... no, I definitely would have thrown you out of my office. But you know something? Recently, I realised we're building a system that ignores all peoples' real needs... and yet we have the cheek to call it a 'welfare state'!"

Paul Prince shrugged and said nothing.

"Anyway, to get back to the interview: what makes you think you're the ideal candidate for this job?"

"Well, I'm probably not the ideal candidate. If I wanted to give you a good answer, I'd need to have a better idea of the kind of person you're looking for... Actually, George, I'd like to know if you're really committed to making the changes you mention in your firm," he asked, staring straight at Lovejoy.

"What's that?" asked the president, taken aback.

Paul never gave up on a question once he'd asked it.

"Are you committed," he insisted, "to changing the things you said you wanted to change here?"

"Well... yes. I reckon we need to make a couple of changes."

"Can I ask you a couple more questions?"

"Um... why not. Fire away."

"Do you believe in the potential of human beings?"

Lovejoy scratched his nose once again. And it wasn't itchy this time either.

"Do I believe in... Of course, of course."

"And in running organisations in a more human way?"

"What do you mean by that, Paul?" The chairman stroked his chin thoughtfully.

"I mean, creating the best possible work conditions for companies to achieve their aims, but also to respect and improve the well-being of their employees."

Lovejoy nodded and pursed his lips. "I guess so."

"And would you be willing to give that job over to the person you hire?"

George shifted in his chair, ran the palm of his hand over his bald patch, and sighed again.

"Well, first of all I'd have to... Let's see..." He was at a loss for an answer.

"What I mean is, in order to change, you have to give up some things, and once you get started there's no going back. It's a matter of faith, isn't it."

"Faith?"

"I mean, trusting in new developments, making way for the unknown..."

Lovejoy stiffened. Suddenly, he remembered the strange, faraway voice he'd heard during his brush with death. 'Trust in what you can't see and you'll begin to feel it... Commit yourself to what you feel and you'll really see it.'

He picked up Paul's CV and went on, trying to regain control.

"Paul, if I hired you, what would you contribute to this company?"

"Mainly, these three things: first, I'd take a detailed look at the general state of things here, and find out how satisfied the people working here are. Then, I'd focus on the essential things in my business strategy; that is, I'd introduce new policies to improve working conditions in the firm. And lastly, I'd give the staff emotional training courses to further their self-knowledge and personal development. Whether I was able to achieve this or not would depend on how much you believe in what I'm telling you.

The chairman took a pink handkerchief out of his pocket and slowly wiped his face with it, covering his nose and mouth. He took a series of deep breaths. "Um, well..." he said slowly. "That doesn't sound too bad, I guess..."

"Would you trust me to do this?"

Lovejoy wasn't used to such direct talk. "This... let me see... I don't know, I'd have to think about it..."

"Do you trust the people who work for you?"

"That's not that easy, you know. There are all kinds out there."

"I don't know if you'll agree with me on this, but I know that you can't take risks if you don't trust. And if you don't take any risks, there's no way you can ever do anything new – it's like sentencing yourself to stay in the same place forever, don't you think?"

The chairman was feeling more and more uneasy. All the interest he'd felt at the beginning of the interview had vanished. All kinds of doubts were running through his mind. Fear, insecurity and mistrust were taking over. They were his lifelong enemies; for fifty-seven years he'd fought change because of them, denying the trust and courage in his heart.

"Tell me, Paul: How much experience do you have in human resources in general, and particularly in making changes in work conditions?" This was a serious question. The chairman slipped back into his cold, distant mode as the businessman who'd led SAT for the past two decades.

"I don't have much experience. But I'm full of enthusiasm and commitment."

This was just the answer Lovejoy needed to justify his decision.

"I'm terribly sorry, Paul, but the truth is, you're not what we're looking for," he lied.

An uncomfortable silence fell. Finally, Paul broke it. "Thank you very much for your time, George ." He got up and held out his hand.

"You're welcome. It was... a pleasure to meet you," said the chairman, shaking it. "You're an interesting chap. I wish you luck."

"Do you mind if I ask you one last question?"

Lovejoy looked away and shrugged.

"What would you do," asked Paul calmly, "if you weren't afraid?"

Silence fell again. An image flashed into the chairman's mind of him pushing a red button under his desk and summoning two bodyguards in sunglasses and dark suits to escort the impertinent Paul out of his office. Nothing of the sort happened, however. And Paul, insistent as usual, continued. "What would you do, George , if you weren't afraid?"

"I don't know what you're talking about," said the chairman, unable to meet his eye.

"Well, if I believe what your advert said, I hope you'll agree that what your firm needs most is a different paradigm in managing the people who work here."

Lovejoy frowned, nonplussed. He wiped the sweat off his forehead with his pink handkerchief. "Different what?"

"I mean, a different way of feeling, talking and doing things here. It might sound crazy, but what I'm offering is a radical change in the way things operate. Isn't that what you were looking for?"

"Maybe; but I don't think this is exactly the right moment for it." Two dark patches were spreading under the chairman's armpits.

Paul Prince walked over to the door. He glanced around the reception at the other candidates and then turned back and said to the chairman, "I hope you find who you're looking for there."

Lovejoy said nothing. He pushed his body back into his chair and put his hands on his head.

Paul crossed the reception to Linda's desk. She quickly hung up the phone. "How did it go, Paul? Will you be staying with us?"

He gave her a gentle smile, which she returned flirtatiously.

"Looks like I'm not the man your boss needs."

Linda's shoulders slumped dejectedly. She sighed. "If it was up to me you'd have been hired. I'm so sorry."

"Don't be sorry. That's the way things had to be. Have a good day, alright?"

He said goodbye and then went down the stairs, passing Bernard Martin.

"So? Was I right or was I wrong?"

Paul shook his head and took off his tie, slipping it into his pocket.

"Bloody sharks!" The concierge grumbled angrily. "Why do the good guys never win?"

Suddenly, George Lovejoy appeared at the foot of the stairs.

"Paul! Wait a minute!" he said. "Listen, the man you were talking to in the office wasn't me. It was the old me. And I've had enough of him. I've made a decision. Would you like to join the firm?"

"I'd love to," said Paul. "I can start tomorrow if you like."

The chairman and Paul Prince shook hands and the agreement was sealed.

"Congratulations. You're our first Human Resources Manager."

"Thanks, George . I want to revolutionise this company. And I have a feeling we're going to have a great time, too."

"Revolutionise the company...?" the chairman thought to himself. "Have a great time...?" Then he laughed. He laughed at his old self.

"By the way," added Paul. "The first thing I'd like to do is give my job a different name. If you think it's okay, I'd like to call myself 'Personal and Corporate Values Manager'."

"I don't know what you think of that, Mr. Lovejoy," interjected Bernard Martin, "but it sounds great to me."

II
SOME BOSSES ARE BAD FOR YOUR HEALTH

Monday 14th October 2002.

Linda Orizio hung up the phone and pulled off her earset, tossing it on her desk. She got up and hurried over to the Machine Room. George Lovejoy had given the room its name years ago, and all of her thirty-eight colleagues worked in there. Each of the staff had their own cubicles, which were separated from the rest by grey panels one metre eighty high. The place was a sort of home to them: they worked there from nine in the morning to nine at night, Monday to Friday, and some weekends too, when they were asked to cover the so-called 'peak periods'. Squeezing in any overtime was hardly possible, and it wouldn't have been paid for, anyway.

No natural light came into the Machine Room. It was a stuffy space with little ventilation. People took some time to adapt to it. The cactuses in the corners were the only plants hardy enough to survive there, though it was hard to say whether they were alive or dead. From above, the room looked like a sort of maze. Anyone who wanted to see anyone else had to stand up, the shorter among them on tiptoe or on their desks. This meant that most of their communication was done by phone.

There was only one office in the Machine Room: Mr. Ian Insley's, the chief consultant. A spiral staircase about four metres high led up to it. From there, Insley kept watch over the other staff. His door was always closed.

"Listen" shouted Linda from the doorway. "Ian is coming back today!"

Everyone suddenly dropped what they were doing, and the room fell silent. Slowly the workers left their cubicles and gathered in small groups to discuss the news. Consultants with consultants. Marketing employees with marketing employees. Accountants with accountants. Computer technicians with computer technicians. The heart of SAT was divided, and nobody seemed to want to take the first step to sew it together again.

In the consultants' group, sparks were flying. There were less than five hours to go for a new service to be presented. It had been especially designed for the firm's most important client. All eyes were on Emmanuelle Evans and Alice Osaka, who were doing the Power Point presentation and report.

"How're you getting on with it?" asked one of the consultants.

"Have you rehearsed your presentation for this afternoon?" inquired another.

"Make sure it goes perfectly, won't you?" demanded a third.

Emmanuelle Evans scratched her ear with her right hand and glanced down at the watch on her left wrist. Then she took off her glasses and started polishing them to gain a few seconds, hoping her colleague would take over and do the answering.

But Alice Osaka was hiding in the Machine Room toilets. She was sitting on the toilet seat, praying that nobody would wonder where she was.

"Everything's under control," answered Emmanuelle after a pause. She folded her arms and stared at the ground. "Um, nearly everything, that is..." The group stared incredulously at her. "Actually, I'm not sure..." Her eyes darted around. "Where's Alice got to?" she finally burst out.

In the other groups something similar was happening. Everyone was blaming everyone else, trying to avoid any responsibility. Survival of the fittest was the way at SAT. The staff had no choice but to compete if they didn't want to be eaten by the only predator in a suit and tie: Ian Insley. He'd been out of the office for the last month; but he was coming back, and they could almost feel his claws on them. He had told them he'd been going through a difficult time, but they had no idea exactly what it was about. Insley was chief consultant and had no qualms about speaking his mind to anyone. As a human being, though, he was incapable of expressing what he felt.

Bernard Martin was sweeping the reception when he saw a man of about thirty-seven walk in. He was large and had a paunch.

"Morning, Mr. Insley," smiled the concierge in surprise. "Haven't seen you in a long time! How are you?"

Without even looking at him, Insley held up his palm and said, "Not now, Bernard. No time to chat, sorry. Long day ahead of me."

Bernard leant on his broomstick and sighed. "Cold-hearted shark," he thought, smarting. "What would it take for him to say hello."

Linda Orizio had been practising a kind welcome back for ten minutes when Ian flashed by her desk with a curt "Good morning." He was gone so fast she had no time to answer. Outraged, she shook her head and frowned.

The staff in the Machine Room were staring hard their computer screens as if completely intent on their work. It was just an act, though. All of them were watching out for their boss, who was striding up to his office. At the door, he stopped and lit a cigarette, puffing the smoke out hard. Luckily for him and unluckily for his lungs, smoking had not been banned at the office.

"Good morning," he said. "I hope you enjoyed the break." He took another puff and then called, "Emmanuelle! Alice! Come into my office now, will you?"

All the rest of the staff breathed a long sigh of relief.

Ian sat down in his tall, large, comfortable chair. Sitting back in it, he smoked his cigarette right down to the filter and then stubbed it out in a white ashtray on his desk. The ashtray had turned a nasty grey colour from so much use and was spotted orange and yellow.

Alice and Emmanuelle, meanwhile, sat down in two wooden chairs, considerably lower than the bosses'.

"Good to see you back again, Mr. Insley," said Emmanuelle politely. "How are you feeling?"

"Very well, thank you," grunted Insley, putting his feet up on his desk. "Doesn't it show?"

Alice Osaka gave a tight shrug and glanced at her colleague, who was carefully polishing her glasses.

"Mr. Insley," she whispered. "Alice and I were wanting to say that... Well, that we've been terribly stressed the whole month. We've hardly had any time to rest and enjoy our life outside the office..."

"That's what I call 'work'," the boss cut her short. He disliked having his authority questioned. Obedience was intolerable. "I'm a serious man, remember? I don't like having my time wasted on nonsense. Can we please take a look at that presentation, now?"

Alice uploaded the file onto his desktop, waiting for Emmanuelle to speak. She, however, said nothing, and finally elbowed Alice, who pretended not to have noticed.

"Well? What this, then? Does Power Point run on its own? Or is this going to be some kind of presentation for the deaf?" asked Insley sarcastically, lighting another cigarette.

Emmanuelle started biting her nails and shifting in her seat. "God, what an asshole," she thought. "I hate this damn job."

She began the presentation.

A few minutes into it, Insley suddenly stubbed out his cigarette and folded his hands behind his head. "Stop, will you," he said.

He got up and, pacing around his desk and staring into the distance, he said, "Let me see. How can I say this without hurting your feelings... I don't always want to be the bad guy, you know that; but if a person wants to be paid for their work, they actually have to do it. Do you really expect us to build up our customers' loyalty with such stale old ideas? If there's anything they can't stand, it's having their intelligence insulted. Haven't you realised yet that they always need to be given more than they ask for? We have to look after them, spoil them. And if keeping them satisfied means sleeping nights at the office, well, we sleep at the office, don't we!"

Emmanuelle tugged at her shirt collar and gave an uncomfortable swallow. Alice sat stock still in rigid silence. Neither of them dared look directly at him.

"Anyway... Nobody can say I don't try. But it's obvious I just can't leave things to anyone else. Like my granddad said, if you want something done well, do it yourself. I guess it's simply about asking people to do what's within their capabilities. Go on, go and do something useful. And I don't want any interruptions until the clients get here, alright?"

Emmanuelle and Alice went back down by the stairs, whispering to each other. He was even worse than usual, they thought. After a short while, the boss appeared in his doorway, and leant out, saying loudly, "Why can't you all be a bit more like me? Jesus Christ! Doesn't anyone take things seriously here?"

Slamming the door, he sat back down on his throne. Annoyed and angry, he pulled his cigarette pack out of his jacket. It was empty.

"Damn!"

He threw his lighter on the ground, enraged, and banged his desk so hard with his fists that the two cigarette stubs bounced out of the ashtray onto the table. Then he sat still for a few seconds. Finally, he started stroking his wedding ring. Pulling it off, he held it gently in his hand.

"I'm so sorry, my love. I've failed you," he whispered. Covering his face with his hands, he groaned. "Why did this have to happen to me of all people? Why me!"

He pulled on the ring again and kissed it sweetly, then burst into tears, weeping quietly so that nobody would hear him.

George Lovejoy, meanwhile, was on his way to the Machine Room. Covering his nose and mouth with his pink handkerchief, he took a deep breath and then put it back in his pocket. He gave a cough as he walked in, and the staff stopped talking when they heard him.

"Afternoon. I'd like your attention for a moment, if you don't mind. I'm pleased to... Um..." Lovejoy took out his handkerchief again and started mopping his brow and neck. "I'd like to introduce SAT's new Personal and Corporate Values Manager."

"What happened to the old one?" someone from IT joked.

But nobody laughed. Everyone was waiting expectantly. Nobody apart from Linda the receptionist had the slightest idea of what was happening.

"Jokes aside... I want you to know that things..." Lovejoy put his handkerchief over his mouth again. "That the way things are run here is going to change slightly. Isn't it, Mr. Prince – I mean Paul."

Paul Prince smiled and took a step forward. For a few seconds, he watched his new colleagues faces. Meanwhile, Ian Insley half-opened his office door and stood silently behind it.

"Good morning. I hope you're having a nice day. My name is Paul, and my aim in this company is to bring about the changes we'll need if we want to build a healthy, sustainable working environment. I honestly believe that not only is happiness possible in the workplace; it's a fundamental right for all human beings. But happiness means living a balanced life. I want you to know that I plan to give you flexible working hours, and as much independence as possible so that you can do your jobs freely and responsibly."

Emmanuelle raised her eyebrows incredulously. Alice Osaka gave a timid smile.

"As you know," Paul went on, "we live in a capitalist system. Capital has become the focus of our existence. But our chairman has decided to stand up and take some risks. SAT is to become a pioneer enterprise and be the first in making the changes that others will make too over the next few decades, bringing in the coming philosophy: humanism. Humanism means making sure you feel good so that you can give your best. We feel that if we can get rid of any obstacles that stop you from being happy here, your creativity and productiveness will increase and our mid-term financial results will improve. To prove our commitment to you, and show you that money is there to serve your interests, and not vice versa, your salary will be raised ten per cent as of next month."

The chairman raised his right hand to his heart. He felt like an attack was coming on. His left hand covered his mouth with his handkerchief again. He inhaled and exhaled deeply, but it didn't make him feel any more relaxed.

"Trust in what you can't see, George" he said to himself. "Just trust in it, will you, for once and for all?"

"Before you leave," added Paul finally, "please go by reception and ask Linda to give you your questionnaire on your satisfaction in the workplace. I'd need you to hand it in some time this week. Ah! And from tomorrow, please dress however you feel comfortable. I'd just ask you to wear suits when you really feel it's appropriate. Don't forget, the changes we'll be bringing in here are aimed at increasing our growth on all levels. And in order to achieve that, we want to help you to commit to your own growth as human beings." He was still smiling. "It might be hard to believe, but we're all much more than we seem to be. As Antoine de Saint-Exupéry said, "What is essential is invisible to the eye."

Up in the doorway of his office, Ian Insley folded his arms. He stared at Paul Prince. "Who the hell does he think he is?" he wondered to himself. "The Little Prince?"

III
MODERN SLAVERY

Monday 24th May 1999.

Three years before his opening speech as SAT Personal and Corporate Values Manager, Paul Prince had been working in the human resources department of one of the most prestigious consulting firms in the world. Nothing in his school record would have indicated he'd get there. He'd always been a lagger. And when he went to university to study Business Management, nobody expected it would get him very far.

Paul was the black sheep of his family. He always wanted to do things his own way, even if he didn't know exactly what that way was. In this, he constantly came up against his father's wishes. His father was a businessman who had insisted that his four children, all of them sons, studied business and then made it their career. His first three sons hadn't put up much resistance. But the youngest one was a harder nut to crack. Paul was different, and the differences in him were treated by his family as faults to be got rid of. This led to a long series of conflicts and difficulties during his childhood and early adulthood.

Finally, Paul gave in. Like many young people around him, he felt lost. He had no inner compass which would lead him towards his true vocation, and so he decided to walk the wide path of resignation and conformism and do what society expected of him. And as soon as he took that road, Paul felt defeated by his greatest enemy: fear. So much so that he would tell his friends he felt 'tormented'.

The years went by, and Paul's inner torment only increased. He knew he was living a second-hand life, and there was no way he could fool himself or act like he wasn't. Much as it pained him to do so, he started searching inside himself. His intuition told him that that was where he'd find the answers he hadn't managed to find outside. So he started living a double life. In the daytime, he worked for a company he didn't believe in, doing things he loathed to do. At night, he threw off his chains for a few hours, reading all kinds of books on psychology and philosophy. And his task in life became the work of finding the path into himself. His only commitment was to find out who he was, and how he could build a full, constructive, meaningful life for himself.

Paul had been working at the same firm for over two and a half years, but ever since he'd set foot in there he'd refused to wear a tie. It was his form of peaceful protest. He'd been told off for it, and his bosses and colleagues had even got angry sometimes about it. But perhaps because he was young – just twenty-seven years old – he was considered one of the most difficult, hard to manage employees in the consulting firm. Rumour had it his days were numbered.

Two of the other men in his department stopped talking when he went in. It was only Monday, but they were wishing aloud that Friday would come. Paul came in at half past ten, late again. His blond curly hair was in a mess and his chin was covered in stubble. He sat down at his desk, leant back in his chair, crossed his legs on top of his desk and let out a long sigh, closing his eyes.

"I don't get you, Paul," said one of the others. "I really try, but you don't listen. How can you just act like you don't care?"

"Lay off, will you? Can't you see I'm working?"

"You? Look... I've had enough of you, Paul. You're bone idle. Can't you see that everything we do in here ends up happening out there? You should be proud of it. Because of the work we do, companies are increasing their profits, earning more and more every year. And how often do I have to tell you that we're the number one firm in our sector! Number One, Paul!"

Paul didn't move or open his eyes, but he burst out laughing.

"What?" said his colleague. "Did I say something funny?"

Paul Prince opened his eyes and stared. Frowning, he said in a hard voice, "I don't know what I'd find more worrying: whether you really believed what you've just said or whether you're just pretending to. In case you didn't know this, the guys at the top only care about you because, in exchange for next to no money and doing slave-like working hours, they're making a profit out of you. We're not building up anything worthwhile here. How can you believe this firm is improving the way others work when we're being treated like a bunch of machines here? Take a look around you. It doesn't matter what floor you work on, it's a jail. They make us believe it's a job, but all it is is a new form of slavery! I don't know about you, but I can't see anyone smiling. I can't see anyone having fun. Everyone here is tired, stressed or burnt out... So why don't you stop trying to fool yourself and everyone else? If you really cared about the world outside, you wouldn't be sitting in here, I'm telling you..."

"You're such an idealist, aren't you, Paul," his other colleague broke in. "Can't you see how competitive the market is? Most of my friends would pay to have the chance of working here... It may not be the perfect place, but what place is? Anyway, what do you expect us to do. We're young, and what else can we do but tow the line? At least I try to make an effort and work hard. That way I know I'll get my reward in the end, a better position."

"And when that happens, what will you do?" interrupted Paul, clenching his fists. "Carry on working even longer hours at your senseless job. Ah! You're right! You'll be higher up on the ladder! And better paid! And more respected! But what good will it do you to be admired? Inside, you'll still be a wreck, wishing for the weekend every Monday... Come on, wake up! If you carry on like this, you'll be like your dad, like mine, like so many others... just another sad man in a tie."

His colleagues exchanged glances, shaking their heads.

"Come on, Paul," said one of them. "You're just pissed off, because you know that people like you never get any higher in the company."

"You probably already know this," said the other, "but you're treading on thin ice here. Haven't you heard what people are saying? You might be out the door soon."

"You know something? I'd love it if they threw me out! If I had what it took I'd have walked out ages ago... I don't know about you, but I need to believe in what I do, to feel passionate about it; I need to feel like I'm part of something useful that gives people something extra. I'm sick of resigning myself to everything. I didn't come into the world to make money. And certainly not at the cost of turning into some vacuous, grey, mediocre version of myself!"

The other two burst out laughing. Paul Prince felt like banging his fist on his desk, but instead he got to his feet and stalked out, gritting his teeth. As soon as he was through the door, the whispering began.

"You know what?"

"I've had enough of him. I think he's lost his mind."

"I reckon you're right. He's always been a bit strange."

"He's going to be out of a job soon. I feel sorry for him, actually."

"Yeah, me too."

"Anyway, we'd better get back to work. I'd like to finish before ten tonight."

"Why?"

"It's my girlfriend's birthday today."

"Couldn't you celebrate it some other day? I heard things are tense with the bosses at the moment."

"Yeah, I heard that too."

"Apparently we're way off the mark this term with our profits. I don't know, I just don't think it's the best time to be dodging your work, do you? I bet you'll thank me for saying this in a couple of years when you're higher up in the firm and we're both earning loads of money. And your girlfriend will be happy, too."

"I guess you're right. Let me call her now and tell her we'll have to put her birthday dinner off."

IV
SUFFERING WILL GET YOU NOWHERE

Wednesday 13th November 2002

Working hours at SAT had been different for a few weeks now. The staff began at nine and worked until two, and then from three to six in the afternoon. There was also half an hour of flexibility at the beginning and end of the day. Insley had not been very happy with the changes, although he'd accepted them; but the rest of the staff were delighted with them. Even so, to date, none of them had left the Machine Room before nine at night.

Early in the morning, Paul Prince sat down in the chairman's office, where he'd scheduled a series of meetings with every single one of the workers in the firm. He was wanting to hear their criticisms, complaints, ideas and other comments, and channel them towards improving working conditions for the forty human beings who worked side by side twelve hours a day, five days a week, forty-nine weeks per year. Listening carefully and patiently, Paul noted down every single detail of what he heard. He listened quietly and sympathetically, saying little except for the occasional question, sincerely interested in the person in front of him and his or her situation. For some reason, the staff felt comfortable and relaxed with him, and most of them ended up telling him what they thought and how they felt.

"I don't want to sound arrogant or overly critical," said one consultant angrily. "But if you want my humble opinion, I find the way things are done here a bit pathetic. Sometimes I feel like I'm the only one here with a bit of intelligence. There's no initiative, no real leadership! All Insley does is shout at us and tell us everything we do wrong and how we ought to improve this or that. He's the most demanding person I've ever come across. It doesn't matter how long I work or how hard I try; it's never enough for him. He always asks for more, he always wants me to do better. And I'm sick of being pushed to commit more and give more but constantly being judged for everything I do. I feel undervalued, like I'm getting the short end of the stick at this company."

"I don't want to bad-mouth anyone," said Linda Orizio, lowering her voice tactfully, "but seeing as you're asking, well, nobody here cares about anyone else. I try to be kind and helpful to everyone, but sometimes I feel like I'm the only one who does. Everyone just thinks about themselves. I can't remember the last time anyone asked me how I was. And nobody thanks you for anything, and that makes me really sad. There's too much selfishness, and I think it's because of the way Ian behaves. It affects everyone else. I know he's having a bad time, but he's the boss, and he doesn't set a good example of how to be generous or helpful to others. I find my colleagues' attitude a bit disappointing. But don't tell anyone, will you? I get on well with them, really."

"The problem is, we just not as good as our competitors," explained a marketing executive in a smart new suit. "Our staff just aren't competitive and that makes it hard to work well in a team. I feel like I'm an efficient guy and I'm good at what I do, but nobody values my work here. The other day I signed a deal with a new client. That means hundreds of thousands of euro. But nobody gave me any recognition for it or even mentioned it later. You see, nothing you do gets noticed. So, seeing as you ask, sometimes I do feel a bit frustrated. But I'm fine, really. It's just sometimes I feel like nobody acknowledges my work, like nothing I manage to achieve means anything. And I don't know what else I can to do to make Ian sit up and take notice of me."

"I think people here see me as an oddball," said a female consultant by way of an introduction. She was wearing a purple dress and purple-rimmed glasses. "I guess it's because I have a peculiar way of looking at things. But I still don't understand why Ian refuses to listen to any of my suggestions. Between you and I, he might do an excellent job as a consultant, but as a person I find him very superficial. Run of the mill, even. I feel like he stops me from being creative. I don't want to sound dramatic, but I feel like I can tell you this: I don't feel like I can be myself at this company. Nobody understands me. And I feel like the rest of the staff ignore me, or are jealous of me. I don't think they can get over me being different or special. Also, I don't like acting against my own principles. However much it costs, I want to be faithful to who I am."

"This kind of personal interview makes me a bit nervous. What I like or don't like is my own business, I think," said a man from the finance department with a stiff face. "But seeing as we're here, I will say that I don't feel like there's any respect for my space or my privacy here. We're all stuffed together like rats in a cage, and I'm not surprised people find it hard to concentrate. I don't like telling tales like a kid at school, but there's so much time wasted by people who play computer games and surf the web when they should be working. You know, people writing emails or chatting to their friends on the computer. And I hear so much gossiping about personal stuff, like we were all out for drinks for something. Frankly, it all gets to me a bit. And sometimes I feel like Insley is watching us from on high. And to make it worse, my cubicle is right below his office."

"I think there's too much pressure. Or maybe not..." Emmanuelle hesitated. "There's always so much work to do, but we're never told how... I don't know, what I'd like is to be told exactly what I have to do and how to do it. That way I'd be able to do whatever is expected. But maybe that's too much to ask... I don't know; I wish someone would stand up to Ian for once. He's the worst tyrant I've ever had as a boss. I think I'm a loyal person, but I've stopped trusting him. And I no longer believe in what I do. There's no direction in this firm any more. Nobody knows where we're heading or what we want. There are no values. I don't know... I've kind of lost hope; I want to leave. I'm not sure yet, though, I may not."

"Everyone is so boring here!" said one of the IT staff. "Yeah, yeah, I mean it. They're all so dull. When I got here I tried to bring a bit of life into the place, to get people to come out to dinner. I organised nights out at bars and restaurants, you know, so that we could have a bit of a drink and a laugh. But it never came to anything. In four years I only got them all together twice. Imagine that! It feels like a graveyard to me. Everyone takes it too seriously. Obligations, responsibilities, that's all they can think about. You must have noticed the atmosphere in the Machine Room. It's horrible, and I'm not surprised. How can anyone feel any different with that ogre of a boss who does nothing but moan and rage at all the staff. I feel less and less motivated. If we can't have any fun then it just makes me want to give up."

"I really hate the way I'm told what to do and how to do it all the time," said a woman from marketing, looking directly into Paul's eyes. "I can't stand being controlled. I really hate not being trusted. I told them when I came to work for them, I need to be given space to breathe and do things my own way if they want me to do a good job. But they didn't take any notice. It's the survival of the fittest here, and all I can do is put up a fight and try to be tough, however much I hate it. It's so good you're here, Paul. If you want me to be honest, this place makes me sick. Sometimes I feel like saying my mind to Ian about the way he behaves and how he treats everyone. And not just him. There's plenty of injustice, plenty..."

Alice Osaka was the last person Paul interviewed.

"I think everything's fine the way it is."

"So there's really nothing we can do to help you enjoy your job more?"

Alice hesitated, then folded her arms and shook her head.

"Very well, Alice. Thanks very much for your help. If there's anything you need, please tell me."

"Thanks Paul. I'll be off now, if you don't mind. I have a lot of work to do," she lied. She gave him a broad smile, but the expression in her eyes told a different story.

Paul had been listening for hours and needed to relieve himself. He went to the men's toilet outside the Machine Room. It was five in the afternoon and all the staff were at their computers. Inside the toilets, he put his notebook down by the washbasin and stood in front of one of the ten urinals. Suddenly, Ian Insley burst in. He chose the urinal next to Paul's and unzipped his trousers. His eyes were red with anger. He'd just had a shouting fit at Emmanuelle Evans and Alice Osaka in front of all their colleagues. The firm's most important client had just phoned him to tell him they'd no longer be needing their services. At least for the time being. Apparently the presentation they'd been offered in October had been below standard.

"You seem like a nice guy," said Insley after a while. "To be frank, your opening speech..." he closed his eyes and swallowed, clenching his fist and holding it to his chest. "Ever since then, I've been trying to see the staff as human beings, with feelings, wishes, dreams, expectations... But I can't. I must be a lost cause. However hard I try they just seem like machines to me... Machines that follow orders and have to achieve certain aims. That's what we pay them for each month, isn't it?"

Paul said nothing.

"I don't know why you bother to give them false hopes," Insley went on. "We both know that you have to be tough on people to keep things running, you know, you've got to stay on top of them. Anyway, it's a bad idea to mislead the workers. We can't make them think we're going to put their needs before the company's aims. That will just complicate things. I wonder if you get me..."

Insley did up his zip and went over to the washbasin. Picking up Paul's notebook, he started paging through it.

"What's up? Nothing to say? Look, Little Prince – let me make something clear to you. I don't want you to get me wrong. You might have fooled the old guy, but you're not fooling me. I don't like you and all your humanistic bullshit. Happiness is for fools! You're wasting our precious time here!" Insley lit a cigarette and took several deep puffs on it. "You might not have realised it, but the world is a giant business now. If we're not strong, if we can't compete, we won't survive. Do you get me, Little Prince?"

Paul put his hands under the tap, giving himself time to respond. "Breathe deep and don't take it personally," he reminded himself. "He's just trying to get a rise out of you. You're here to help, not to fight."

"I'm not trying to cause problems at SAT," he finally replied calmly. "I don't know what you think Ian, but if all of us row together in the same direction, all of our lives will be improved, and that will lead to a mid-term rise in profits for our company."

"What do you mean, 'our company'? Don't get the wrong idea here, will you? You're a new recruit. I've been here for the last thirteen years. Plus, Little Prince, this isn't a rowing team. Write this down in your magic notebook, will you? 'Ian Insley will head his boat wherever he wants.'"

Insley threw Paul's notebook on the ground. "I like things just the way they are. Get me? And in case you didn't know, Little Prince, I'm the one in charge here, not you. Me, not you! Alright?" He was huffing and puffing angrily as he spoke, fuming like a volcano about to erupt. All he needed was an excuse to blow his top.

Keep calm, Paul, try to accept it, he doesn't realise what he's saying, a voice insisted inside. He's doing the best he can, in the only way he knows...

"I'll take good note of what you say, Ian," he answered clearly.

Insley looked at him in surprise. That wasn't what he was expecting. He wondered if Paul was being sarcastic. "Are you trying to take the piss out of me, Little Prince?" he said angrily.

"Just take it, Paul. Don't let him get a rise out of you, it won't get you anywhere," the voice inside Paul insisted. "Try not to say anything that'll blow his fuse."

Just then, George Lovejoy came in, humming sweetly.

"Look at you! My two most trusted men in here together!" he joked.

This time Ian wasn't the only one who kept quiet. Paul was sunken in thought and didn't answer.

"Well, Ian, have you passed on your thoughts and concerns to our Personal and Corporate Values Manager ?" asked Lovejoy.

"I have, don't worry. I just told him exactly what my values are... they're all in there, in his notebook," replied Insley, looking down at the ground. "Well, I gotta get rowing," he said, slapping Paul's back and winking. "As I said, count on me if you... need anything." Paul Prince took a deep breath, picked up his notebook, and then asked Lovejoy if he could have a word with him.

"Sure," said the chairman. "Come and see me in five minutes. I'll be in my office." Before Paul could leave, he said worriedly, "Is it good or bad?"

"That depends on how you look at it," answered Paul.

In Lovejoy' office, the chairman invited Paul to sit down and tell him whatever he wanted. He folded his hands and added, "Well, what is it, then?"

"I was wanting to talk to you about the labour satisfaction questionnaire."

George took his pink handkerchief out of his pocket and held it in both hands.

"Fire away," he sighed, half-closing his eyes.

"I have some really good news," Paul smiled, taking out the sheet with the results on it.

"What? Good results? What do you mean?" exclaimed Lovejoy, dropping his handkerchief on the desk in front of him.

"Well, according to the interview, ninety-nine percent of our staff are very unhappy here," said Paul. "Only one person refused to answer the questionnaire, because, according to him, 'Happiness doesn't exist.'"

Lovejoy was stunned. "But what have I been doing in all these years of directing this firm?" he wondered, folding his hands on top of his head."

Paul let the chairman take his time.

"It's a waste of time regretting things, George ," he said after a while. "What's important is what you can do now, what we can do together. But one thing is very clear: if we carry on the same way, we'll get the same results." Paul paused. "Think for a moment: how do you think we're treating our clients, if all our staff say they're unhappy?"

The chairman frowned and stared down at his desk, shaking his head. Seconds later he raised his eyebrows and stood up. "Our biggest clients are our staff. It seems so obvious to me now, but I'd never really thought about putting it into practice," he admitted.

"That often happens, George. The truly important things in life are so important we forget about them."

Lovejoy wiped his face slowly with his handkerchief.

"That's why I'm telling you that this is really good news," added Paul. "The best thing about knowing we've hit rock bottom is that the only way from there is up – wouldn't you agree? What we need to focus on now is providing the best possible working conditions for our staff..."

"...Because the more we look after them, the more they'll look after our end clients, right?" added George.

"Right. We need to make sure there's nothing in the way we do things that makes them feel like victims," said Paul. "Wherever there's an outside excuse for them to justify their own dissatisfaction, they'll waste time and energy blaming others for it. They're already doing that. Nearly all of them told me that their lack of motivation and low productivity is because of the unpleasant environment they have to work in. And as for Ian, I heard the word 'toxic' more times than I can tell you."

"'Toxic'?" frowned the chairman.

"Yup. That's it. A lot of them said that working at SAT is bad for their mental health... I really think it's time to build a better working environment. If we do that, then the workers will realise that in the end, they're the only ones who're responsible for how they're feel. And that's the main idea I want people in your firm to grasp."

"*Our* firm, Paul. We're a team now."

Paul smiled.

"To get things working creatively in our firm and start innovating, we need to help our workers approach their working day maturely, freely and responsibly," he went on. "We have to start helping them to be happy. There's nothing more unproductive or unsustainable for a company than suffering. And I tell you, those people are burnt out, they're fed up. Most of them have forgotten why they're here and what they're actually working for." He nodded towards the Machine Room. "If you think they're the company's first client, then you have to act like they are. And it's up to us to take the first step."

The chairman threw his pink handkerchief in the bin, and walked up to Paul.

"You know what?" he whispered. "Go ahead and do whatever it takes. I trust you."

Back in the Machine Room, Emmanuelle Evans quietly stood up on her tiptoes to check what everyone else was doing. Her watch said it was past six, but nobody else had made any move to leave. All of them were staring at their computer screens. Most were surfing, chatting or playing Patience. The only one who wasn't was Alice Osaka, who had fallen asleep at her desk.

"You can do it, Emmanuelle, go on," she urged herself. "Go on, be brave, be the first one to leave. They'll all follow you, you'll see. No, no, no. Don't be crazy. Just stay put, you don't want them to badmouth you. Come on, what do you care what other people think. It's six o'clock and time to go home..."

She picked up her belongings and strode firmly towards the door, but after three metres she turned back and sat down again at her desk. "No, best wait and see what everyone else does," she concluded. And that was that.

Half an hour later, Paul Prince walked into the Machine Room. Straight away he noticed how the staff were looking over at one another, each of them waiting for the next one to leave so they could do the same without being slandered, and glancing up at Ian Insley's office in case they were being watched.

Paul made an announcement. "I'm planning to organise an introductory course in self-knowledge and personal development," he said. "It's entirely voluntary, of course. If you're interested, ask Linda for the details and we'll find a date that works for everyone. I'm going home now, so enjoy your afternoons!" And just before he left the room, he added, "By the way, Ian isn't in his office at the moment. He's taken the afternoon off to spend time with his wife."

In less than five minutes, the Machine Room was deserted. It was the first time the staff had ever left before nine at night. Unfortunately, they were so excited they forgot all about Alice Osaka, who woke up hours later, bewildered.

V
THE TRUE SCEPTIC EXPLORES THE UNKNOWN

Saturday, 11th January 2003

One Saturday, the Machine Room was turned into a space for a course on personal development. Three rows of chairs were set up around a whiteboard at one end. All the staff at SAT, including George Lovejoy, came. He sat in the first row, next to Emmanuelle Evans and Alice Osaka, who was dressed for the occasion in a long white and yellow dress. On the other side of him was Linda Orizio, the receptionist, who was wishing she'd dressed a bit smarter. Even the cleaning staff were there, and Bernard Martin, too, who was trying to cover up his excitement.

Ian Insley was the only one who'd refused to come.

"Self-knowledge and personal development are a load of nonsense, food for the weak!" he'd screamed a couple of days before at the office. "I don't understand how people can be taken in by that stuff, happiness, inner peace... It's absurd, stupid, a waste of time!"

Nobody dared voice the feeling, but they were all glad he wasn't there. What they did say, though, was that ever since Ian had come back to work he'd been more bad-tempered than ever. They all knew how explosive he was, but he'd never behaved so arrogantly or tyrannically as he was doing now. Lovejoy took note, and admitted that lately, Ian had been coming in and out of the office 'in a horrible mood.'

"He hasn't told me much, but I do know that something is wrong with his wife... That was why he was off for depression," he disclosed. "I've known Ian since he was a little boy, and he's my right hand man now. But if he carries on like this I'm going to have to do something about it." George was staring at the ground as he said this. He couldn't believe what he'd just said.

"Good morning, all of you, and thanks very much for being here. This is the first part of our course in self-knowledge and personal development," began Paul Prince. "We'll be following up on it next month, so that you have time to put what we learn into practice.

HONESTY, HUMILITY AND COURAGE

First of all, I'd like to congratulate you for being honest with yourselves. I find it truly admirable of you to invest your time, your will and your energy in your own personal and professional improvement. Normally, people fight to change what is outside them, and blame others for their own problems, acting the victims in difficult circumstances, and even complaining about the hard things that happen to them. It's not often that we'll admit that we are the co-creators of our problems or will take responsibility for them. Whenever we do, we get closer to finding the solutions we were searching for outside ourselves. Looking at ourselves in the mirror is the hardest thing to do. Sometimes it might be hard to see this - but the roots of our own suffering, and also our happiness, are inside us, not outside.

'The fact that you've come here today out of your own free wills also shows you're able to be humble. This is an essential attribute for anyone who wants to grow and evolve as a person. The wonderful thing about humility is that it opens the doors of our minds and hearts to learning and transformation. Particularly because humility rests on the principle that we don't know things, but are willing to learn them. And that's amazing. So thank you to all of you.

'Also, as you've probably guessed, looking inwards means journeying into the unknown, and that often causes a lot of fear and insecurity. So I also want to thank you for your courage and bravery.

'Another thing I'd like to mention,"' he went on, "is that your attitudes here are the key towards us using this time usefully and helpfully for all of us. So don't believe anything I tell you. I'm quite sure you'll agree that society has filled all of our heads with more than enough beliefs, and we don't need any more added to them in this course. As far as you can, please try to test out what I tell you here. Put it into practice, and analyse the results. Words and ideas are very useful for showing the path to experience, but they aren't the same thing as experience itself. The aim of this course is to encourage you to commit to putting theory into practice and coming to a better understanding of things through your own experience. There's a Madagascan saying that goes, 'You can be told what a baobab fruit tastes like, but you'll never know what it's like until you try it yourself.' The bridge between knowing and not knowing is experience and understanding - not what you're told, or what you believe. Don't believe anything. But do test everything out. That's the only way to find out whether the information you're given will be true or useful for your personal growth.

'And a third crucial point: everything we'll be talking about here is related to highly intangible aspects of the human condition. That means that all of you will have to become scientists. What I mean is, that the laboratory where things are discovered, revealed and transformed in this case will be your inner selves. This is why personal growth is also called 'the inner science'. I also want you to understand that when you hear something new or unfamiliar, the most common reaction is defensiveness. It's a conservative reaction, and it's precisely what will block your development and evolution. So I'd ask you to become true sceptics, to explore the unfamiliar. Doing so will lead you to new experiences that will give you an understanding of things you didn't know before. Your age, your personal circumstances are of no importance here. All you need to do if you want to broaden your knowledge and wisdom is to defeat a subtle, but tenacious enemy: the arrogance of thinking you know it all. It will close your minds to new ways of learning.

'And finally, I must remind you that self-knowledge in the western world began with the aphorism 'Know yourself.' This was spoken in 6 BC, and it's older than the history of philosophy itself. The search for inner knowledge might be in fashion right now, but it's been around since the times when the great wise men, like Zarathustra, Mahavira, Laozi, Buddha, Socrates and Jesus of Nazareth, spread their knowledge among their disciples... Religion made myths of them; but they were all philosophers, and today we consider them to have been the first men to teach of and specialise in personal growth. Any questions?'"

WHAT IS SELF-KNOWLEDGE AND WHAT IS ITS PURPOSE?

Nobody said anything, so Paul Prince went on with his presentation.

"Very well. So, what is self-knowledge? And how can we use it? In order to answer that, I'll begin with one of my favourite stories. It's a Sufi fable." He smiled. "'One night, Nasrudin was staring at the ground and walking round and round a lamppost. A neighbour went walking by, and asked him, 'Have you lost something, Nasrudin?'

'To which Nasrudin replied, 'Yes, I'm looking for my key.'

'His neighbour started searching around with him. After a while, another neighbour walked by. 'What are you looking for,?' she asked.

'We're trying to find Nasrudin's key,' they answered.

'And she bent down and started searching with them.

'Some time later, another neighbour appeared. Together, all of them combed the ground for Nasrudin's key.

'Finally, one of the neighbours, who was tired and longing for his bed, asked, 'Nasrudin, we've been looking for your key for hours now. Are you quite sure this is where you lost it?'

'Nasrudin shook his head.

'So where did you lose it, then?'

Nasrudin straight away answered, 'I dropped it somewhere inside my house.'

'So why are we searching here for it, then?' asked another neighbour, mystified.

'Nasrudin looked them in the eye and said, 'Because my house is very dark, and there's a lot more light out here.'"

'A thoughtful silence fell in the Machine Room. Finally, George Lovejoy exclaimed, "I got it, Paul! I've been searching around with my eyes closed my whole life! If I understood you right, self-knowledge consists in searching for what we want inside ourselves. And that's precisely the last place we've been taught to look."

"That's it, George . Self-knowledge is the gateway to our inner selves, and that is where we can connect with our own well-being. And perhaps, if we haven't been there for a long time, opening the gate might make us feel afraid. But as our eyes grow used to the dark, we'll find it easier to move around. It's the only way to discover who we really are. And to find that out, we have to know how our minds work: how we can manage our thoughts at will; how we can regulate our emotions constructively; what the true cause of our unhappiness is; what the path to a balanced life is; and in general, how to live a full, meaningful life in our current working lives, with their high speed, stress and tiredness... The learning process is full of treasures and surprises, and will help us to relate to others more intelligently, fluidly and harmoniously... It might seem hard to believe, but success isn't the key to happiness. In actual fact, happiness is the key to success."

"I can testify to that," said the chairman. "I have no doubts about it any more. The answer is inside, not outside."

"Why has no-one ever told us that?" asked Emmanuelle Evans. "I've never heard of any kind of instruction manual for the human condition. But maybe I just don't know about it – maybe there is one and I've just never encountered it."

Alice Osaka raised her eyebrows, shrugged and stroked her stomach thoughtfully.

"Not only have we never been taught to look within ourselves," said Paul, "but society has conditioned us to focus everything, even our own obsessions, on what happens outside us. We tend to think happiness will come with more money, with success, prestige, a new car, a prettier or more handsome partner... and that's exactly what desire does: it makes us chase after what we don't have, thinking that the things we want will bring us the happiness we don't enjoy in the present. But on the way, we lose the only thing we need, and what we already have: ourselves, that is, our own inner well-being. Let's go back to Nasrudin. The paradox in the fable is that first we have to search underneath the lamppost, in the light, before we realise that the key we're looking for isn't there. That will show us that we have to shift the focus of our attention, to turn inwards and look within ourselves. As hard as it might seem, sooner or later you have to look in the mirror. That is an encounter you can't put off forever.

'As to whether there's an instruction manual, well, yes, there is. Not only one, but many of them. There are a huge variety of tools for personal growth. All of them are different paths to the same place: knowledge and understanding of the human condition, ways to get back in touch with our innate wealth: happiness, balance and inner well-being. Each one of these tools is like a map of the human condition: they help us to see the steps we need to take more clearly, the steps to our own inner light. And once that light is turned on, there's no need for the tools any more. We can make our way in life freely and independently.'"

IS SELF-KNOWLEDGE SELFISH BEHAVIOUR?

Linda Orizio was listening carefully. "But if self-knowledge consists in finding happiness by looking into yourself, doesn't that mean it's selfish?" she asked, delicately patting her hair.

"It might seem hard to understand at first, but self-knowledge isn't an end in itself," replied Paul. "Learning to be happy within ourselves is the first step in the journey, not the end of it. Knowing ourselves is just a way of getting to understand ourselves better, and helping us to set things straight inside ourselves. So we need this kind of conscious selfishness to be able to live with our own selves in peace. We want inner peace, joy and trust to predominate in our lives instead of anger, sadness and fear. Also, healthy, sustainable well-being allows us to lovingly serve other people."

"Lovingly serve others?" grunted Bernard Martin defensively.

"Well, when you're happy and at peace with yourself you can start feeling the same way towards others and about your life. Being a well-balanced individual makes you a better parent, a better brother or sister, or executive, boss, work colleague... By 'better', I mean more aware, more objective. What I found was, until I was twenty-seven, I was really unhappy inside, and I had all kinds of issues with my family, particularly my dad and three older brothers... But recently I've realised that I wanted to be understood and accepted by them and didn't think of trying to understand or accept them first. I hadn't learnt to love myself, so I wasn't able to love others either." Paul Prince paused and looked over at Bernard unflinchingly, smiling at him. "And when I say love, Bernard, I don't mean the feeling of love. I mean behaving lovingly. Loving means understanding, accepting, respecting, thanking, considering, listening, giving, and generally, in being kind to others whatever the situation. If you think about it, you can always find a way to be kind."

"You're right, Paul," nodded the concierge.

"Why aren't we kinder to each other, then?" asked Alice Osaka in a near-whisper. "Why are we so inhumane, so cruel and insensitive towards one another?"

The rest of the staff couldn't remember the last time they'd heard Alice speak, and listened in quiet surprise.

REACTIVITY IS SLAVERY

"Interesting questions," said Paul, and Alice smiled. "If we all take a close look at the way we work, we'll find that all our attitudes and negative forms of behaviour happen mechanically, impulsively. None of us ever chooses to get angry or to feel sad or afraid. I've yet to meet someone who would prefer to suffer than be happy... And let's say you get angry with someone and shout at them - the first person you harm is yourself, isn't it. The paradox lies in the fact that it's we ourselves who create the anger we feel; so feeling it is something like taking a sip of cyanide. Just think of how you feel after any kind of emotional conflict with someone, even if it's just inside your own mind... The best thing to do is when you wake up each day, remind yourself that no negative emotion, or thought, or attitude, or negative form of behaviour will ever bring you anything positive, beneficial or constructive. And not only that. Negativity destroys you; it breaks down your immune system and makes you much more vulnerable to all kinds of disease. Be careful with it; it's pure venom.

'And the fact that we sometimes behave toxically and poison ourselves is only due to us not being in charge of our own emotional reactions and letting them be set off without us even noticing. When reactivity is our main mode of being, we become victims of circumstance. We become so used to our own psychological imprisonment that we mistakenly conclude that the way we feel is caused by the way things work around us. Luckily, we can learn to stop being reactive and become proactive. And this is precisely one of the aims of self-knowledge and personal development. It's a matter of understanding *why* and learning *how*...'"

"Um, Paul..." Linda put up her hand. "I see exactly what you mean with reactivity. You see, in my work as a receptionist I come across all kinds of people, and many of them aren't exactly interested in personal development... Sometimes I get people on the phone who just won't give up, or are rude to me, or sometimes even insult me. And I know that when they get rude they bring out the absolute worst in me. I normally end up getting angry or sad, or both. But when I was listening to you, I realised I don't choose to feel those emotions. Sadness and anger appear reactively in me. And I really do experience it as a sort of psychological imprisonment; sometimes it takes ages for me to start feeling better..."

"Yeah, some people take days, years or even their whole lives!" joked one of the technicians in the back row.

Linda laughed shyly. "But Paul, what I don't quite understand is what it actually means to be proactive. I've always thought it just meant showing initiative, but it seems like it's something deeper than that - right?"

CONSCIOUSLY TRAINING TO BE PROACTIVE

"Thanks, Linda, for sharing your experience with us. Noticing how we react is the first step to getting over it. As you said, reactivity is an impulsive mechanism. We don't choose it, so we can't be responsible for the consequences of it either for ourselves or others. And it's true that there are people who live with it all their lives," he added, winking at the back row. "But as I was saying, luckily, being proactive is the flipside of being reactive. Proactivity is the ability all of us have to take whatever happens to us healthily and constructively. Let's continue with Linda's example. There's an external stimulus, for instance, someone being rude to us, and then there's an internal reaction – anger or sadness. But in between the two, there's a space where we have the liberty to choose the most convenient response, for ourselves and others. That space is what we call 'consciousness'."

"'Consciousness'?" echoed one of the cleaning women, writing it down in her notebook. "Nice word, isn't it."

Paul smiled. It was one of his favourite words.

"If we live consciously," he said, "we can decide not to get upset when things happen that would normally upset us. You see, it's not what other people say that upsets us. It's how we react to it. If we stopped reacting, we wouldn't make ourselves upset. And this is a power we can work on by being proactive. To go back to Linda's example again – one thing she could do would be to remind herself that she might not agree with what the other person is saying, but that person has every right to be rude. And not only that: she could also try to understand that whenever a customer is rude to her, the first person they're harming is themselves. As I said before, it's as if they'd taken a sip of cyanide... And if you think that, then you can empathise with whoever it is, and understand they're not in charge of what they're doing or saying, and that they're harming their own selves with their attitudes and behaviour. That is, by being reactive, that person is not being responsible for what he or she is doing, and that means there's no need to take it personally. They would probably be rude to whoever crossed their path at that moment... But I do realise all of this is very easy to say, and the real challenge is how to put it into practice and start learning from our mistakes. Like everything in life, getting satisfactory results depends on your own commitment and training."

Paul Prince paused briefly, then went on with his explanation.

"I'd like to share with you a revelation I had a couple of years ago. There was this friend who was having some problems, and he asked me if I could look after his dog. The dog's name was Grassy." The audience laughed. "I said I would, but obviously, I just didn't know how to train her to fit into her new routine in my flat. The day after she came to stay, I woke up in the morning to find she'd gone to the toilet on my rug. I was furious. I yelled at the dog and told her never to do that again. Half an hour later I was still fuming, and I had no choice but to clean up the stinking mess, which, obviously, was still sitting there immune to my complaints. Anyway, I went off to work, still quite irate.

'Next day, I woke up and the same thing had happened. There was Grassy's little turd sitting on my rug. I got angry again, and had to pick up the mess, and went off to work in a bad mood. As you can see, it wasn't what she'd done that had made me angry. It was my own impulsive reaction whenever I saw it sitting there on my living room carpet. She stayed with me for several weeks and every time I thought about how she was soiling my carpet with her turds, I got annoyed. Anyway, one morning, I woke up as usual. By then I kind of expected to find the turd sitting there, because there was nowhere else in the house I could put the dog. But when I saw it with my own eyes, I smiled. In fact I laughed. I realised Grassy had been messing on the same corner of the rug every day. She'd made it into her own private toilet... I cleaned it up as usual, and Grassy looked at me with her tail between her legs. But this time, I stroked her. And then I went off to work in a really good mood. That day, I realised that my experience, that is, what I feel inside, isn't so much a result of what happens to me, but of how I interpret it, and the attitude I take on towards what happens..."

The audience stopped laughing and sat thoughtfully, glancing at each other without knowing exactly what to say or ask.

REALITY AND THE WAY YOU INTERPRET IT

"Let me give you another example," Paul went on. "I'd like you to imagine you're watching Barça and Real Madrid play. The match is just about to end, and nobody has scored any goals yet. Suddenly, one of the Madrid players runs into the Barça penalty area, slams into one of their defenders, and falls down. The referee calls a penalty for Madrid. How do you think the Barça fans would react?"

"They'd start booing and shout that it's not a penalty, that the Madrid player fell down on purpose. And they'd worry they were going to lose the match," said the Barça fans among the audience. One of them was quite indignant.

"What about the Real Madrid fans?"

"Just the opposite," said another of the workers, a Real Madrid supporter. "They'd be really happy and sing away, and say that the Barça player deserved it, that it was clearly a penalty... no doubt about it!" He smiled cheekily.

"But if you think about it, the external fact is the same," remarked Paul. "You could say it's neutral or objective. But the way each of the fans interpret reality, what happened, is completely subjective, and it depends on their beliefs, and the desires and expectations they identify with. When I say 'identify with', what I mean is, what are the kind of things we think ought to happen in order for us to be happy and feel good? Anyway, half of the fans will have seen a clear penalty and will be feeling great, while the other half will totally disagree and feel outraged. The funny thing is, if the Madrid striker finally misses the shot and the game goes the other way, so will the feelings on each side switch completely."

Paul then intuitively decided it was time for a change of tack. He needed to talk less rationally, more creatively.

"What I'm going to do now," he said, "is to draw something for you. It'll help me show you the difference between reality and our interpretation of it." He drew a silhouette on the whiteboard, then turned and smiled at the audience. "Tell me, what do you see here?"

Some people answered, in disappointed, sarcastic voices, "A hat."

And Bernard Martin added, "After everything you've told us, how can you possibly ask us something so obvious?"

Paul Prince couldn't help smiling. Adults, unlike children, always need things explained, he thought to himself.

"Have any of you read *The Little Prince*?"

Nearly all the staff raised their hands. Even the concierge knew the book. And Paul, who never let go of a question once he'd asked it, insisted. "Try to remember then, what do you see here?"

Silence fell. Suddenly, one of the cleaning staff exclaimed, "It's a boa constrictor, isn't it! Yeah, and it's digesting an elephant, right?"

Bernard Martin shook his head, wanting to laugh. He wasn't the only one. But only a few of the audience, including George Lovejoy, would admit that the drawing did, in fact, show a boa constrictor digesting an elephant. The rest of them sat still, like the hat, concealing what was inside them...

"Sorry to interrupt, Paul," said Emmanuelle Evans, "but, just out of curiosity, I'd really like to know what this has to do with our day to day working lives?"

"Well, if you manage to apply it, quite a lot," he answered. "If you take a good look at what our interpretation of reality depends on, then you see that the true cause of our well-being or unhappiness is not so much what happens to us, but how we see it, how we interpret it. And it's precisely that, our interpretations, that generate the negative emotional reactions that do us so much harm inside, or the conscious, proactive responses that can do us so much good.

'Here's an example: once, I was walking around a town in Madagascar when suddenly it started raining. And then pouring. Harder and harder. It was like the sky was coming down on the earth. So I went to shelter under a market stall, and I found a group of tourists there. The interesting thing was, while the Madagascan fruit and fish sellers were cheering and feeling grateful for the rain, the tourists started cursing their luck. Their plans for the day had been interrupted and they didn't like that. And yet the same rain was falling on everyone, wasn't it? You might say it was a neutral, objective part of the day, like there are neutral objective parts of your working day. But the Madagascans reacted to it happily, whereas the tourists complained and felt victimised by it. And if you analyse this in more depth, then you realise you can't change or control what happens to you – when it starts to rain, say – but you can change your attitude towards things like that, and cultivate a healthy, constructive, proactive attitude instead of a poisonous, destructive reactive one. Right?"

George Lovejoy nodded thoughtfully. The rest of the staff sat in silence, absorbing and processing all the information their teacher was so generously giving them.

THE TYRANNY OF EGOCENTRICITY

Paul Prince turned to the whiteboard. On it, he wrote, in capital letters, 'EGOCENTRICITY'.

"This here is the real key to the whole issue. Egocentricity is the basic cause of all human suffering and all our common problems. It makes us prisoners of our own reactivity and continual victims of our circumstances. It also makes it really hard for us to develop proactive attitudes, and because of that, to responsibly take on the best attitude or behaviour in any circumstance. And that means that without making a conscious choice, dissatisfaction and unhappiness take over in our daily lives. Because the more selfish and egocentric we are, the more impulsively, the more negatively we end up behaving every time something we don't like happens... and that means, frequently, doesn't it?" Bernard Martin nodded emphatically.

"Well," said Paul, "egocentricity, the cause of so much pain and conflict in all of our lives, is the consequence of living under the tyrannical rule of two of our worst enemies. One of those enemies is ignorance. That is, not knowing who we are, what we need, and how we can relate more peacefully and harmoniously with others. The other one is the lack of conscious awareness, which is, not wanting to know, looking the other way, without being aware of the consequences of our thoughts, attitudes and behaviour on our own selves and the people we spend time with.

'If you think about it," he went on, "many of us, if not nearly all of us, are ecogentric: we always want reality to fit into our expectations, our desires; and we feel awful when it doesn't. And instead of realising that we're the only ones responsible for what we experience, we normally play at being victims, blaming others, or life itself, for what happens... So much so that humans are said to be the only animal that will stumble over the same stone, not twice, but thousands of times over. And blame the stone for it, too! What could be more childish than that!"

"Paul," said Emmanuelle Evans, who was writing it all down in her notebook, "could you give another example of egocentricity?"

"Let's see... Egocentricity is driving out in the morning and taking it for granted that all the other cars will let us through at a crossing, won't drive across in front of us, or won't brake suddenly when we're behind them. I say 'taking it for granted' because if they don't let us through, or if someone drives across in front of us, or brakes suddenly, we react negatively. Sometimes we get angry, or even shout, and that way, we start the day off on a bad note... But the interesting thing is that whenever it's us who won't let other drivers through, or drive in front of them, or brake suddenly, then we find an excuse or reason to justify what we've done. So when others do it to us we take it as a personal affront, but doing it to others is a simple mistake, a slip-up, or minor accident, and there's always a way to justify it..."

"*Touché*," smiled Lovejoy. "I guess the opposite of egocentricity is living more objectively... Traffic is what it is, you can't change it, can you? So the best thing to do is adapt to the way others drive. That's something we can do."

"Yes. I mean, in the end, we're all just doing the best we can, aren't we?" added Linda Orizio, winking at Paul. "I do try not to brake on purpose to annoy whoever's behind me. If I don't do it, why should other drivers?"

Bernard Martin raised his hand and joked, "Wow, Paul. I thought it was only the rich and famous who could afford to be egocentric and selfish. This course is really making me think. Now it's me who doesn't know who I am, or where I'm going - or anything at all!"

The audience laughed, and so did Paul.

THE POWER OF ACCEPTANCE

"I know exactly what you're feeling, Bernard. What's happening is that your old beliefs are being shifted. But don't worry – it's just a stage in the process of getting to know yourself. We have to throw off what we know in order to build something new. Or, in other words, if you want to learn you first have to unlearn... What we're seeing here is how to become more efficient managers of our own selves and work on relating better to the things that happen to us. The biggest challenge we will ever face is the challenge of accepting others as they are, and going along with the flow of things as they happen. And by the way, acceptance isn't the same thing as repression, resignation, or tolerance, even. And it has nothing to do with weakness, laziness or stagnation, or not caring about things. Just the opposite... True acceptance requires wisdom and profound comprehension, and it means no longer reacting impulsively, and beginning to respond effectively to people and circumstances. The things we won't accept are the sole cause of our reactivity, that is, our negativity, unhappiness and suffering."

"The things we won't accept are the sole cause of our suffering," echoed Emmanuelle Evans aloud as she carefully wrote it down in her notebook.

"Good idea to write it down, Emmanuelle," said Paul. "I'd encourage you all to repeat that a hundred times each day to yourselves, morning, noon and night. You can say it to yourselves as you leave for work, or pick up your kids at school – or when you have to meet your boss. As you know, bosses are often great teachers. They might not realise it, but they help us to develop as people."

Every single one of the workers thought of Ian Insley. And for the first time ever, many of them did so with a touch of sympathy.

"Acceptance helps us to maintain our own well-being and inner peace," added Paul. "If we accept things, we stop simply reacting and become able to consciously select our attitudes and behaviour. That's what taking responsibility means. And I'd like to remind you once again that, as in any other concept of personal development, learning to accept never comes out of intellectual comprehension. No – it's like a muscle you develop by using it every day... Understanding the meaning of acceptance, and the benefits it gives you, basically requires training. Do you all understand me, or are there any questions?"

A quick coffee break was then had by all, after which they went back to their seats.

The concierge raised his hand. He'd been sitting with a frown on his face for some time. "Let me see, Paul," he said. "Before you go on, there're a couple of things I'd like to ask."

"Go ahead."

"I've been thinking about everything you've told us, but I still can't quite work it out. Are you trying to say that I have to accept that others can be rude to me or treat me badly? Are you telling me I have to take such negative behaviour from others? Because personally, I'd find that really hard, and right now I see no motivation at all to do so."

"That's a very interesting point, Bernard," said Paul. "But the paradox is that we're not trying to change our reactivity for others, but for ourselves. And the reason is that in time, being so egocentric and playing the victim becomes a vicious circle where fear, anger and chronic sadness lead to depression..."

THE FUNCTION OF EXISTENTIAL CRISES

"But what often happens," he continued, "is that we're so resistant to change that we only dare question the way we think when our pain becomes unbearable. Which means, Bernard, that suffering is the most common way that people learn. It's the way to what we call our 'existential crises': psychological processes that shift the foundations of our beliefs and values, bringing about new levels of consciousness."

"I know what he means, Bernard," said George Lovejoy. "As you know, I had that near-death experience, and ever since then I've been going through a deep crisis, and it's changing me from top to bottom..."

Paul gave a smile. "Do you think I'd be here if it wasn't?"

There was a burst of laughter all round. George also laughed.

"Anyway, to go on with what we were saying," said Paul, "I just want to point out that the biological function of suffering is to make us feel our belief systems are ineffective, that they're blocking our capacity for fulfilment. That's how adversity and suffering put us in touch with our own need for change and evolution – with honesty and humility, and the courage to break out of the limitations society has set us in and forge our own way through our lives.

That's why they say that existential crises are the best chances we get in life to stop fooling ourselves and break free of our own 'comfort zones'. But this kind of crisis has nothing to do with your age, culture or social status. No – they're there underlying the existence of anyone who doesn't feel happy or satisfied with their life. Reality is a great chance to dare to grow, change, evolve, and above all, to take responsibility for our own lives, our decisions and the consequences of them... And that's what we call 'maturity'; it has nothing to do with your real age, it's your psychological age – true experience is a question of learning and transformation, not of how long you've been alive."

Bernard scratched his chin. "So," he mused, "what you're trying to tell me is that every time I feel afraid, or get angry or sad, I'm the one who's creating the negative emotions inside me? Is that it?"

"Right. It might be hard to accept at first, but you're the only one responsible for what you experience. You're the one who creates your own feelings, in any circumstance, towards any problem, and so you're the only one who can solve it... Because it isn't about changing what's outside, but about transforming what's inside, which is something we all can do. Little by little, day by day, by knowing ourselves, by understanding and accepting ourselves, we grow and evolve, and change our way of looking at and interpreting everything that happens to us."

Then Emmanuelle Evans raised her hand. There was something that had been running around her head for a while now.

"Why do some people never learn from their suffering?"

Almost everyone in the room thought straight away of Ian Insley, their boss in the Machine Room.

WHAT EXACTLY CHANGES WHEN YOU CHANGE?

"There's one thing we know, and that's that the biggest thing stopping us from learning, growing and evolving is the way we tend to get stuck in the role of the victim. It's a totally ineffective attitude, but there are those who claim it's the dominant philosophy in today's world. The truth is that there are many people who refuse to admit that they are the ones responsible for what they feel and for the way they manage their lives. Many psychologists even say that most people are not in touch with their inner selves. That's why it's so hard for us to look inside, and why we tend to search for evasion, take drugs, or seek entertainment to desperately fill the existential void inside us. But as we've seen here, these are unconscious, ineffective, unsustainable attitudes. Nobody can escape from him or herself forever. The strange thing, though, is that even though many people aren't leading fulfilling lives, they're so scared of change that they're not brave or confident enough to step out of their comfort zones and would rather take refuge in them than break out of them."

Bernard Martin scratched his chin again. "Well, it's hard for me to admit, but I do think there's a sort of coherence in all this. To be frank, part of me finds it scary and even annoying to think that it might all be true..."

"Thanks very much for your sincerity, Bernard. But don't worry about how you feel right now. It's all part of the process. I'd like to point out here that the more we develop inside, the wiser and more objective our way of relating to our circumstances becomes. We stop relating negatively to the things that happen. And that makes us gradually happier. A new state of well-being emerges, which was already inside us, but which we lose contact with when we accumulate too much pain and suffering."

"Excuse me, Paul," said Alice Osaka, "but could you tell me what exactly changes when someone changes?"

"Their paradigm."

It wasn't the first time George Lovejoy had heard the word, but he'd never quite understood it. Before he could ask, Bernard Martin reactively interjected, "Their what?"

"Their paradigm. Meaning, the way they look at, understand and act in the world. A change in paradigm is a profound revelation, like something shifting inside your mind. Some people call it 'the awakening of consciousness', because it brings a new understanding and puts us back in touch with our essence as human beings, with what really matters. Changes in paradigm are the bridge between seeing ourselves as victims and taking responsibility. When we truly take responsibility for our own experience, we regain our lost enthusiasm for building our lives moment by moment, as children do. Children are masters in the art of living. But strange as it seems, as adults we can learn to do this consciously. Once we get over the limitations our mind has been conditioned with, we realise we have the ability to use the entire breadth of our imagination and see things differently. And that's when we can enjoy life with our hearts. That is actually the essence of any game. The great difference between children and adults is that they allow themselves to play, but we don't."

VI
THE PATHOLOGY OF SUCCESS

Thursday 24th June, 1999

Four years before Paul Prince's course in self-knowledge, he had found personal growth and everything related to it completely ridiculous. His reaction whenever he saw anyone reading about it was to demonize it. He thought self-improvement literature was just a form of escapism, a way of evading reality. But the way he thought was nothing but a symptom of his deep inner unhappiness. At the age of twenty-seven, he still hadn't learnt how to be happy or feel peace within himself. And so he struggled against others and the world outside.

Feeling grumpy and exhausted from his day's work, he was the last to arrive at the Prince family dinner his father had organised. That night, they were celebrating their mother Vicky's birthday. Paul, her husband, had been fighting to keep her memory alive among their four children for the past nine years. But between each dinner course he'd drink down three beers, a whisky on ice, and half a bottle of red wine. Next day, he'd follow up the tradition by waking up sad, tired and hung over, with blurred memories of the night before.

Paul, at the time, was at war with his family. For years, the only thing he'd felt he had in common with his other brothers was their surname. Greg, James and Sebastian were thirty-three, thirty-one and twenty-nine years old. Greg was an accountant. James was an estate agent. Sebastian was a commercial lawyer. All three were married and religiously paid off their mortgages every month. Paul hated the world of finances, didn't believe in marriage, and was strongly against taking out any kind of mortgage, as he believed they were a 'subtle, perverse form of slavery'. Emotionally, he was so different from his brothers that even a simple conversation about the weather was an uphill struggle between them.

As he opened the living room door he heard a round of applause from his father and brothers. His father was on his third beer.

"That's my boy!" exclaimed Paul Prince. "Late and in his waiter's uniform, just how I like it."

All four burst out laughing crudely. Paul gave a long sigh and shook his head.

"I wonder if tonight," he said, "you could try to hold back a bit. I'm really tired, and I don't feel like I can take all the usual stuff."

"Paul's getting pissed off, Paul's getting pissed off, Paul's..." they chorused.

"What have I done to deserve this?" he thought to himself.

He sat down at the dinner table. There was a minute of silence in memory of his mother. After that, they dug in ravenously to a lasagna bolognaise.

"Paul," said his father, "I want you to congratulate your brother Greg. He's just become an important businessman. He's been appointed finance director at work. That means a big raise. How about that, eh? He'll even have his own secretary. Let's make a toast to him, shall we?"

Greg raised his glass and nodded, looking down his nose at his brothers.

"Thanks, Dad. It took me a bit longer than I'd hoped, but now I have everything any man would want: money, success, and a wife who waits for me to get home every night for dinner. All that's left is for me to pay off the rest of my mortgage, hopefully before I'm forty, and then..."

"Don't ask so much of yourself, Greg – you'll make it hard for your brothers to live up to the same standards!"

Then Paul Prince sat silently and looked over at his younger son, who was getting edgy, feeling the next question coming on.

"Now, what about you, Paul? Don't you think it's time you started improving your prospects, becoming some kind of manager? You can't imagine how happy it'd make me."

"Dad, that's probably not going to happen." Paul looked straight back at him. "Happiness is a product of things money can't buy, I think."

"Oh god, don't start," said James, rolling his eyes. "We all know you have different values. When will you stop going on about being happy, looking for meaning and all that stuff. Couldn't you just act like you're having a good time with your family and let us get on with the party? If you've had a bad day, why don't you just shut up about it? Welcome to the real world, Paul."

"What do you mean, a bad day!" Paul retorted angrily. "All I've done since the moment I got out of bed is work at something I don't believe in! And when I get home I'm a mental wreck, and all I feel like doing is watching the crap on TV so I can forget how awful my life is."

"So what are you complaining about?" shouted his father. "That's life, isn't it! I've been working for the same firm for over forty years now! And I've more to go!"

"I mean, what do you think life is all about? Just doing whatever you want?" said James. "Come on, we're in a capitalist system, haven't you realised, not the Little

Prince's planet or something! Why don't you just make a bit of money and have fun at the weekends? You never change, do you? How can you be so naïve?"

"If your mum could hear all this," whispered Paul Prince, "can you imagine how sad she'd feel about you?"

"Don't bring Mum into this, will you?"

"How did you turn out as such an oddball?" his dad insisted. "Look at all your friends from university. They're the same age as you, and they've all been working hard for years and building up their careers. They're married, some of them even have their own flats... Can't you just live like everyone else and be normal?"

"Dad, I know you won't understand this, but living a normal life is the problem, not the solution," said Paul.

"Oh, I knew it wouldn't take long for the philosopher to come out," mocked his father, and the other brothers laughed. "Lucky I didn't let you study philosophy or psychology, isn't it. Where has all that reading and mulling over things got you? What kind of world do you live in?"

Paul's heart was beating rapidly and there were tears in his eyes. Suddenly, he stood up.

"I didn't want to talk about any of this, because of Mum. But I don't care any more. I'm sick of you all, sick of you and your mediocrity. I'm going to leave my job. I want to stop living like a slave."

An excruciating silence fell. Paul got up from the table and headed for the door. His three brothers sat gaping, lasagna bolognaise in their open mouths. Paul Prince was the first to react.

"What! Have you gone mad? No way! Don't you know how hard life is? Have you no idea how difficult it is to find a good job these days? And how am I supposed to face all my friends with my son on the dole? I won't allow it!"

But Paul was stepping out the door.

"Well, you'd better start getting used to the idea. From now on, nobody is going to tell me how to run my life."

Outside, he raised his head and looked up at the stars. "I wonder if the stars are lit so that everyone can find their own one?" he thought, smiling. It was the expression of a man who had taken his first step to freedom.

VII
LEARNING IS THE MEANS AND THE END

Saturday 8th February, 2003

"I'd like to welcome you to Part Two of our introductory course on self-knowledge and personal development," announced Paul Prince. Next to the whiteboard was a very full rucksack. "And also to thank you all for your willingness to learn and grow as people. It's a true pleasure for me to be here with you again. Like last time, I want to ask you to please not believe everything you're told. As far as you can, I want you to check all this information against your own experience. As you know, personal growth has little to do with intellectual understanding and everything to do with what our hearts tell us."

The audience smiled wordlessly. Once again, they were all happy to see that Ian Insley hadn't bothered to come. He couldn't believe his staff were all willing to go through the 'stupid brainwashing session' again. Particularly because they'd decided to go on their own free wills, and on a Saturday at that. And it's true to say that he'd probably have ridiculed what Paul said anyway, or got defensive.

Ian's negativity was beginning to stand out against the rest of the staff's attitude. George Lovejoy wasn't quite sure what to do about it. For the time being, he'd decided to focus on improving working conditions for everyone at SAT. That way he could put off the inevitable personal improvement plan that Paul Prince had designed especially for Ian Insley. Paul had been wanting to tell him about it for days, but George had managed to avoid him. Although he didn't want to think about it too much, he knew that sooner or later he was going to have to take some kind of action. It wasn't that Lovejoy was being careful or respectful. The problem was, he was afraid of confronting Insley. In the end, it took several months for the chairman to take a stand. The worst was still to come...

"Over the last month, you must have had the chance to take a better look at your emotional reactions and how you're able to respond to your circumstances more consciously and constructively – right?" asked Paul. "Before we go on, does anyone have any questions or anything to say?"

Linda Orizio patted her hair, raising her hand shyly.

"I have to admit," she said, looking into the audience, "that over the past few weeks I've been taking a good look at myself, and I've found out for a fact that I'm...

hyper-reactive. Every time a customer doesn't treat me as I'd like, I react negatively. And it's the same at home, with my parents, and with my close friends. I really thought I'd taken in everything you told us last month, Paul, but I haven't been able to help getting angry or sad. And sometimes I've realised that it wasn't what other people said to me that upset me; it was how I interpreted it. Lately I've begun to see that nothing can harm me as much as my own thoughts. But it hasn't done any good. I just can't break out of it, Paul. I'm still a slave to my emotional reactions..."

Paul Prince walked over to Linda, put his hand on her shoulder and gave her a sweet smile. Looking gently into her eyes, he said, "Congratulations, Linda."

"Congratulations? What for?"

"For being so humble."

"But what good does being humble do if I still react to everything?"

"Because that's precisely what will allow you to go beyond your reactions. You see, it doesn't matter whether you react to things right now. It's neither good nor bad. It's just a part of your gradual process of change and personal growth. Just think of how many years of unawareness, reactivity and inertia you have behind you... Consciousness, you see, is like a muscle. If you want to get where you're aiming then you have to have the correct information and then use it by training ourselves constantly. It's like any other learning process. Nobody is born knowing anything. It takes practice, you have to make mistakes and carry on practising. And gradually, naturally, in your own time, you get better at the art of living consciously. In time, you'll develop your own muscle so strongly that it won't be so hard any more to respond proactively when things get difficult. And so reactivity and its toxic consequences will gradually fade out of your life. Also, it's not a linear learning process, you have to realise that. It's sort of circular. Sometimes you have to take a step backwards to take two steps forward..."

TAKING RESPONSIBILITY

"The most important thing about what you just said," Paul went on, "is that instead of playing the victim or blaming everyone else, you're taking responsibility for the anger and sadness you feel inside. And that's a wonderful act of consciousness. How many suffering people do you think will take responsibility for their suffering? Not many, I can tell you. It takes a lot of honestly, humility and courage to stop fooling yourself and face your own ignorance and lack of awareness. So congratulations! Taking responsibility towards yourself is the first step towards achieving true freedom, the freedom that has nothing to do with your outer circumstances. The freedom I'm talking about here is something you experience inside. You find it when you manage to break through your mental limitations. The most important of these is the belief that your well-being depends on things outside you. As Linda showed, that's a lie. Our happiness depends solely on ourselves, on the way we interpret things and our attitude towards our own fate. That's something we have to work at daily. And it has a lot to do with living consciously. That is, with really valuing what we have, with learning from what we go through and enjoying every moment."

Linda Orizio smiled and nodded. "Thanks," she said.

"Thank you, Linda," he replied. "Anyway, let's go on..."

"Wait a moment, Paul," interrupted Bernard Martin. "I don't want to be sarcastic, or to contradict you. But I'm asking out of... well, humility. What do you mean by 'fate'?"

Paul Prince smiled. Bernard certainly knew how to hit the nail on the head...

"'Fate' is all the situations we go through in our lives. It has a lot to do with how we think, how we are and how we behave in the present. We might not know exactly what's going to happen to us, but we can decide to learn from it. When we understand our responsibility to do so then we become aware of the fact that life is a school, and we humans are students that have come into it to learn three things: to make ourselves happy instead of suffering because of things we can't even change; to feel at peace instead of reacting to everything that happens; and to serve others, to stop being selfish and to give the best of ourselves in every single situation and to everyone else.

'And not only that. What we will learn in this wonderful process is that our lives aren't ruled by luck, randomness or coincidence. Synchronicity is the ruling principle. Everything that happens has a reason and a purpose. But like everything important, it's not something that can be seen with the eyes or understood with the mind. It's a profound, invisible network of connections that can only be intuited and understood by the heart. You see, when you stop struggling against life and make peace with it instead, you realise that coincidence doesn't exist: everything has a cause. That is, everything that makes up our lives is ruled by the 'law of cause and effect'. We reap what we sow. And with that, you get rid of the danger of senselessly victimising yourself. It's nothing new, either. People have been repeating the same universal message for thousands of years. But please, Bernard, don't believe a word I say. Test it out. I'd invite you to open your mind and let yourself play and explore like a child. That's the attitude of all real seekers of the truth."

Bernard sat pensively. He had doubts, but decided not to voice them and to let Paul continue with his session.

"Anyway," said Paul, "let's go on now. What we want to do now is to detect which emotions appear inside us reactively, so that we can discover the thoughts that cause them. I'll remind you here that emotions are neither good nor bad; so instead of fighting them, we ought to look at them as what they are: useful information for understanding our belief systems better. So, let's have a look at the three big conflicts that arise every time we interpret what happens to us egocentrically. While you listen, try to see which of them sound more familiar to you..."

ANGER, FEAR AND SADNESS

"There's a kind of person whose initial impulsive reactions tend to be mental. If you're that kind of person, you're afraid of having a bad time, of suffering. You're scared of not being able to face problems or overcome difficulties, and of having demands placed on you or being betrayed by others. And you worry about not being able to control your fate. You search for support and direction in order to trust and feel secure and be able to face the uncertainties of existence. You're often overwhelmed by fear, anxiety, confusion, cowardliness, mistrust, indecisiveness and insecurity..."

Emmanuelle Evan's face turned bright red. Her ears were burning. She stared up at the ceiling.

"And then there's another kind of person. If you fall into this category, most of your impulsive reactions occur at gut level; viscerally. You often feel that others are aggressive towards you, and interpret things as if they were against you. You want to be independent, to make your own way freely in life. You don't like being told what to do. You're oversensitive and live on the defensive, and often hold back from conflict. But anger, rage, aggressiveness often take over; irritation, repression, antagonism..."

Nobody said a thing. But all of them, including the chairman, were thinking of Ian Insley.

"The third kind of person's impulsive reactions are emotional," Paul went on. "If you're one of them, you try to please others by developing a false image. Your biggest aim is to be liked and accepted by the people around you. It hurts you not to be considered; you need others to value your company. And you hate not getting any praise or getting no recognition for what you do. You need to feel noticed. And if you aren't, you become sad, desperate, fall prey to emotional dependence, melancholy, disillusionment and feeling like failures. All of this shows up your lack of self-esteem."

Paul paused for a few uncomfortable seconds. George Lovejoy and Linda Orizio shifted in their seats. They felt like he was talking about them.

"During the course, we'll be taking a look at what's behind each one of these inner conflicts," said Paul. "But for the time being, I'd just like to insist on the fact that this kind of impulsive reaction and the sadness, fear and anger that come with them, are a result of us interpreting the things that happen to us egocentrically."

WHAT IS THE EGO, HOW DOES IT WORK, AND WHAT IS ITS FUNCTION?

"These reactions tell us a lot about ourselves," he went on. "But they're also a part of our emotional survival mechanisms; that is, what is commonly known as our 'personality', or 'ego'. This is something like a black cloud that stops us from seeing clearly, and separates us from our true essence, which is what we need to stay in touch with if we want to find the balance and happiness we seek outside ourselves.

'Let me put it differently, and that might help you relate this to everything we've talked about so far. Our egos are the part of us which is unconscious, mechanical and reactive. Being under their influence is like having to see through a pair of glasses that limit and condition everything we see and distort our interpretations of reality. So if we don't understand how our survival mechanism works, we end up being ruled by our own egocentricity.

"Excuse me, Paul," interjected Emmanuelle Evans. "Could you tell us how the ego is formed, and also what we use it for?"

"Of course, Emmanuelle" he said. "As you know, animals have a physical instinct for survival. When danger threatens, they get defensive, or ready to attack, or they flee in order to stay alive. Well, humans have our own survival instinct, too. But because we're so complex, we also have an emotional survival instinct: our egos. We have it because of the extraordinary potential we all have – that is, our consciousness of our own acts. Unlike other animals, we can not only, let's say, have a drink of water: we can decide how to do it – in little sips, or in a glass, or we can choose to splash our faces with it or throw it at someone else. Because we're conscious beings, we can choose. Not only how to drink water, but also how to think, how to interpret what happens to us, what to do with our lives... As we saw the other day, we're the co-creators of what we are and what we do with our lives, and that makes us responsible. This, then, is true creativity: making our lives into works of art."

"Creativity is making our lives into works of art," whispered a consultant, who occasionally jotted things down in her notebook.

"But," said Paul, "whereas most animals can look after themselves soon after they're born just by letting their survival instinct take over, human beings need a long time to do so. And before we become emotionally and physically self-sufficient, we need to shelter behind our emotional survival mechanism. We can only really transcend our egos once our brains are fully developed, which is what allows us to become conscious of what we do, and therefore to become responsible for our own attitudes and behaviour and aim for the freedom I was telling you about."

'As soon as we're born,'" he continued, "we all go through a similar psychological process." He held out his right arm, closed his fist and added, "Like other beings in nature, we're all born as a seed, with a potential in it which we develop during the course of our lives." He pointed at his fist. "The seed is what we essentially are. It contains everything we can become. But when we live unconsciously, little by little, the seed becomes wrapped up in its own ego, a mechanism which is a part of its very essence, whose job is to help us emotionally survive the abyss of our existence. However much love and shelter our parents give us, in the first few years of our lives we develop a series of traumas, all related to the tragedy of coming out of our safe, secure maternal womb. These are feelings of rejection or abandonment, fear, shame, rage, sadness, impotence, blame... All of these emotional wounds cause us so much pain that we hide even further inside the shell of our ego and completely disconnect from our true essence. It's said that the first three years of our lives mark us so deeply that we need our entire lives to get over them. But self-knowledge and personal development make the inevitable process of integration shorter, faster and also more interesting and more gratifying.

'So, little by little we start identifying with our egos. And what they do is to develop a series of impulsive, reactive behaviour patterns whose function is to protect and defend us from the world around us. They also work to get others to pay attention to us and get our parents to love and care for us more. As we've seen, living unconsciously stops us from realising what we need to survive emotionally. It makes us dependent on external factors for our well-being and happiness, for instance, on our relationship with our parents.

"But in time," he went on, "babies grow into children, and that's when the ego emerges more clearly. A child will 'bomb' someone at the swimming pool, and then get out and shout 'Mum, mum! Did you see what I just did?' But his mother might be talking to a friend and not take any notice of him. And that will make the child frustrated. Or, shall we say, it'll set off a negative reaction in his ego. Rather than just having fun and enjoying himself on his own, focusing on what he can do, he's located his happiness in something that doesn't even depend on him: his mother looking at him and telling him how well he did. And that, to put it in a nutshell, is what happens after years and years of sheltering behind our egos.

'In time, we grow up, but continue to follow our unconscious ego patterns: we continue to let our self-esteem, trust and inner peace hinge on things outside ourselves which we can't control, and to forget that happiness and well-being are already inside us. And not only that. Our egos, which we think of as our personalities, are the holders of the beliefs and values society has conditioned into us. In our ignorance of our true, essential identities, we mistakenly believe we *are* our personalities. As you know, etymologically, the word 'persona' means 'mask'. Living behind a mask might shelter us and it might make us feel more comfortable or secure, but it carries a feeling of chronic dissatisfaction and prevents us from being happy and loving other people. The fact of our conditioning means being ourselves is something like a heroic struggle."

"I totally agree with you," said George Lovejoy. "Society's become like a theatre where we all walk around with masks on. We don't know ourselves and we don't know anyone else either! God! I had to reach death's door before I realised I've been wearing a mask my whole life! How is it possible that most of us end up living so completely distanced from our own essence?"

THE DIFFERENCE BETWEEN INNOCENCE, IGNORANCE AND WISDOM

"That's just a part of your psychological process. It's what makes it so necessary to search for the truth – your own particular truth, of course -" said Paul gently.

"Experts in personality psychology say that our identities are created in three different stages. The first stage is known as the state of *innocence*. We go through this stage from birth until the age of seven, eight, nine or ten years. It all depends on how wide awake each child is. When babies are born they're like a blank page: clean, pure, unlimited and unprejudiced. Everything they come across is new, and everything amazes them. That's the treasure of innocence. Just think of most adults' expression when they see kids playing. We smile and the grey cloud that distorts the way we see and interpret reality fades away for a moment. We're taken back to and reminded of the astonishment we once felt and still long for. Children remind us we can be happy at any time. They teach us that the secret is in our attitudes, the attitudes we choose. They don't think, they don't feel like they have to get anywhere in particular; they just play! To grow and evolve, we have to learn to accept reality as it is, marvelling at everything it gives us and reaching back to the child we once were. This is something all the great mystics have been telling us for centuries."

The audiences' faces lit up as they connected to the child in themselves.

"But," Paul went on, "children will believe anything. It doesn't matter who says it or how it's told to us. We just believe things because we're innocent children, and we don't have any references to compare with or question the information we're given. We lap up everything we're told, we absorb things like sponges, but we aren't yet able to discern what might harm us. Some people say that the greatest crime against humanity is contaminating the mind of a young child with false beliefs that will prevent him from making his own discoveries in life. You see, one thing is to condition, but quite another thing is to educate. Conditioning makes slaves of us, whereas the ultimate aim of education is to free us. One of the etymological meanings of the Latin word *educare* is 'to bring from darkness into light'; that is, 'to bring out what is inside us, developing our human potential'. What parents ought to be doing is not projecting their view of the world onto their children, but helping their children discover their own particular way of looking at, comprehending and enjoying the world. If you think hard about it, what sense does it make for our children to *have to* study law or business if what they really love is art or social projects? What sense does it make for them to *have to* work from morning to night at a job they detest in order to earn a lot of money and gain others' approval? Why should they *have to* be Christians, Jews, Muslims, Hindus or Buddhists if they haven't chosen to be? And what sense does it make for them to *have to* follow a path laid by others when what they want is to discover their own one?

"As we grow up, what happens is that the seed within us gets buried under a thick layer of tarmac laid by society." Paul paused. "But then, we go on to the next stage in the construction of our personalities: *ignorance*. Ignorance begins at puberty once we've formed our system of beliefs. Certain messages and ideas we heard during childhood as to what we have to be, do and have in order to be accepted as 'normal' individuals by society, finally end up turning us into what we think we are. Unfortunately, some people get stuck in this stage and never get out of it. Many people find the idea of change so frightening that they prefer to live with the pain, emptiness, sadness and anger of never being who they came into the world to be. 'Some people grow five thousand roses in one garden... yet they don't find what they're looking for... And yet what they're looking for could be found in a single rose, or a little water... But the eyes are blind. You have to look with the heart,' added Paul, paraphrasing Antoine de Saint-Exupéry.

"The third stage is what we call *wisdom* and it begins on the very day we decide to look into the mirror and question the beliefs society has built into us. This will shake the foundations of our false idea of our own identity. Self-knowledge and personal development can help us become conscious of our belief systems, so that we can retain what we like and what is useful and convenient to us, and replace our old beliefs with new information. At this point it becomes extremely important to confirm the truth or falseness of the dogmas we're taught. Lies feed the ego and its suffering, whereas the truth will nourish our essence, filling our minds and hearts with joy, peace and love. The journey of personal development consists in awakening our sleeping consciousness and discovering how our egos work. When we can stop feeding them, we can regain contact with our essence and start enjoying life fully."

George Lovejoy was growing more and more curious by the minute. His mind was full of questions that only his heart could answer. Paul knew this, and played with words to help his students find the path to the answers, a path that only their own experience could reveal.

HAPPINESS AND INNER PEACE GO TOGETHER

"Now that I can see how I became who I was for fifty-seven years of my life," said George Lovejoy, "I have something else to ask you. How can we know when we're interpreting reality with our ego, as opposed to interpreting it with our essence?"

"Well, there's a very simple premise that you can use," said Paul. "Health, satisfaction, well-being and happiness are our essential states, whereas illness, dissatisfaction, unhappiness and suffering are unnatural. If you take that as your starting point, all you have to do is listen to the signals your body sends you, and you'll know whether you're in tune with what is true and natural, or what is false and unnatural. Reality, as we've seen, is neutral and objective. Every time we feel emotions like fear, anger and sadness, it means we've interpreted things egocentrically, that is, wrongly. Let me give you an example: we all know that if you put your hand in the fire it'll burn you, right? Well, physical pain is a signal that fire is harmful to our physical body. The same goes for emotional suffering. Unpleasant feelings are reliable indicators that our way of seeing, understanding and interpreting reality is wrong, meaning it's unproductive and unsustainable. They tell us that the way we're seeing things is harmful to our emotional health. That's why suffering and illness are such important learning processes – they're a way of learning how to tune into our true natures, into lasting well-being and happiness.

"What difference is there, Paul," said Alice Osaka, raising her hand, "between pain and suffering? Aren't they the same thing?"

"No, they're not," he replied; "and it's important we learn to differentiate between them. Let's say, for example, that Bernard got sick of being here, and he got up and punched me in the face. Obviously, I'd feel pain. Right?"

"Don't give me ideas," joked Bernard, and they all laughed.

"Well, pain is inevitable – but suffering is optional. Being punched will physically hurt me. But whether I suffer emotionally from it is a different thing. My ego might react and I might get defensive and want to punch him back; I could easily get angry and channel my anger towards Bernard aggressively. But, as we've seen, what ends up being important is not what happens to us, but the way we interpret it, our attitude towards it. If I become consciously aware of my responsibility, that is, of how I am able to respond, then I could simply accept being punched, pay no attention to what happened, or even laugh about it. In that case I'd have decided to put up with the pain and chosen not to suffer from it.

"Or let's say I have a headache. I could curse and complain about it, or fight against it, making myself suffer. Or I could simply accept that I have a headache, take an aspirin and lie down. Pain, as you can see, is always something physical, whereas suffering is always emotional: we create it inside our minds and it leads from the way we think about what happens to us. So, whether we choose to accept this or not, suffering is a personal choice."

Paul called a break and everyone went off to stretch their legs. After that, they came in again and sat down. Linda Orizio was the first to raise her hand. She wanted to read out a question she'd written down during the break.

"Paul, there's something I can't quite understand... If everything that happens to us is neutral and objective," she read, "and our true natures will lead us to well-being and happiness, then why do people – me above all – insist on interpreting events egocentrically even if it means we continuously harm ourselves in the process?"

QUESTIONING YOUR BELIEF SYSTEM

"Thanks, Linda. I reckon you just hit the key to the whole question." Paul smiled at her and she blushed. "As we've seen, unpleasant feelings are a consequence of negative thinking. Suffering has nothing to do with what actually happens to us; it's a result of how we think about what happens. That means that we should focus on the way we look at our circumstances and interpret them rather than on changing the circumstances themselves. So for instance, if our boss doesn't support us, or doesn't respect us or acknowledge work we've done, and we feel angry, sad or afraid because of it, what's happening is that we're interpreting his behaviour egocentrically. As I said before, we suffer when our desires and expectations aren't fulfilled.

"Let me take that a bit further and answer your question. It's interesting to realise that egocentric interpretations of what happens lead from a series of mistaken beliefs that restrict us. As we saw, we're conditioned from birth by the influence of our parents, in particular, and society, in general, and that ends up creating a set of beliefs in us. It's like a suit that covers our ego. And in spite of all good intentions, such belief systems are based on the ignorance and lack of consciousness of generations... Behind any unpleasant feelings is a limiting belief which also conditions the way we see, understand and interpret what happens to us..."

"Could you give us an example?" asked Bernard. "I'm not completely getting you, I think."

"Sure. We tend to think we'll be happy when things go well for us. Would you agree?"

Bernard nodded.

"Well, that makes us focus on everything that happens outside of ourselves: we try to succeed at work, we want others to think well of us, and we try to get everything we want. But why do we do all that? The reason is that there's a wrong, limiting idea in our belief systems: that is, that our happiness depends on outside circumstances. But the paradox is that things will only start going well for us once we learn to be happy in ourselves, and that comes with a firm commitment to our own self-knowledge and personal development. Which inevitably means questioning our beliefs, which in actual fact are second-hand ideas, norms, values and conventions..."

Paul paused, then went on. "Also, questioning all that will lead us to the truth."

"Sorry to be so insistent," said Bernard, and some people sighed, "but you've mentioned 'the truth' several times, and I want to know what you mean. What exactly are you talking about?"

"By 'truth' I mean whatever information that will give us the results we want when we put it into practice. There are as many roads to the truth as there are human beings in the world. In personal growth, the truth is happiness, inner peace, love..."

"You mean behaving lovingly, right?" said Bernard with a wink.

"Right. This reminds me of when I was in Colombia. I spent a long time there, studying under the philosopher Gerardo Schmedling, who taught me a great deal. He always said that 'The truth is any thought which will bring your mind peace and harmony, and any act that will bring your heart peace and harmony.' The truth, then, is born of your essence, whereas lies are born of your ego. If you want to understand which of them you're choosing at any given moment, all you have to do is look at how you feel inside. Our biological being is very wise. All we need to do is learn to understand it and listen to it.

'Behind every experience of well-being is comprehension and wisdom. With anyone else and in any situation, if you're able to perceive what happens to you more consciously and objectively, you'll find the way to interpret it in such a way that you can preserve your balance. It's only that inner change that will allow you to choose the correct attitude and behaviour at any time. That's what makes it so important to question everything you've been told and free yourself of the lies that might be contaminating your belief system.

'To go back to what I was saying before, then – it's not your bosses' lack of support that makes you feel afraid. It's not his lack of respect that makes you feel angry. And it's not his lack of acknowledgement for what you do that makes you feel sad. The truth is that everything you're expecting others to give you, and life to bring to you, is what you're not giving yourself. You're the only thing you need! Do you feel confidence in yourself? Do you accept and respect yourself just as you are? Do you value and acknowledge everything you do?"

Most of the audience shook their heads.

DARING TO GIVE YOURSELF WHAT YOU NEED EMOTIONALLY

"I'd like to insist on something here," said Paul. "Because of what we lack inside ourselves, we tend to easily believe a very prevalent lie: in the system we live in, most of us think our happiness and well-being depend on external factors. It's a fallacy, one that severely restricts us. Everything we really need and search for outside ourselves is actually within our reach, but within ourselves, and it's in what we tell ourselves each day. And that is what you can give yourself emotionally. The secret lies in detecting the erroneous beliefs that restrict us. In order to do that, we have to be conscious, and become responsible for the interpretations that make us feel bad. That's the only way to replace them with truths we can verify with our own experience – truths such as the fact that our well-being and happiness depend solely on ourselves and the way we interpret things. Wise men have repeated time and time again that the true battle is not fought without, but within, inside each one of us..." Paul Prince ran his hands through his hair, took a deep breath and cleared his throat. "Any more questions?"

Linda Orizio hesitated, then raised her hand. "Just one thing. I understand that everything you're telling us is just theory, and the real challenge is to put it into practice... But I still find it really hard to accept that other people might not think well of me. What can you advise me to do?"

"I completely understand you, Linda. Relationships are the cause of most of our emotional conflicts. We often find it hard to accept other people's image of us, although that image is based on their own values and beliefs. But there's not much we can do to control it. It's part of what is known as the *worry circle*; that is, everything that doesn't depend on us. Our *circle of influence*, however, is everything that is within our reach. In this case, it's how we see ourselves. And that's the only thing we need to focus on to be happy. Every morning, then, we should exercise that by telling ourselves as soon as we get up that our self-esteem, confidence and inner peace depend only on ourselves, not on anyone else.

"If you're not convinced yet, listen to this: when I was in the Peruvian Amazon, I met a shaman, and he told me this tale.

'A man and a woman go on a journey with their twelve-year old son. The son rides on their donkey. They go through a village, and people say, "Look at that nasty boy, riding on a donkey while his parents walk beside him." So the woman says to her husband, "We can't let people talk like that about our son. Why don't you get on the donkey?" Then they go through a second village, and people say, "Look at that selfish father, riding on a donkey and making his wife and son pull it." So the husband and wife decide that the wife should ride the donkey and the father and son hold the reins. And at the next village, people say, "Poor man, he must have been working all day, and now he has to pull the donkey while his wife just sits on top of it. Poor child, too, with such a mother!" The family decide they should all ride the donkey and off they go to the next village. There, people say, "Look at that awful family – people call donkeys beasts, but what about them! They're going to break the poor thing's spine!" So the family get down off the donkey and decide to walk beside it. And at the next village they hear, "Look at those three idiots! Walking next to a donkey instead of riding it!"'"

The course was coming to an end. Finally, George Lovejoy raised his hand and spoke from his heart.

"I just want to say that I've realised that I'm still a babe as far as self-knowledge is concerned." It came out so spontaneously that it caused a giggle all round. "I wanted to ask you, what else can I do in my daily life to become more aware of the beliefs and subjective interpretations that hem me in, and stop being so reactive?"

THE IMPORTANCE OF CULTIVATING YOUR VITAL ENERGY

"Thanks, George ," said Paul with a smile. "To answer your question, let me first point out that all I've done so far is give you information. That is, we've been talking about the importance of being conscious in order not to suffer under our own egos. But another key point in personal development is the need to cultivate our vital energy, which is what will help us maintain an optimum level of consciousness.

'Imagine, for instance, that you wake up in the morning and don't have time for breakfast. You set off for work and on the way, you can't stop thinking about a meeting you have in the afternoon, where you'll have to present an important report to one of your best clients. When you get to work you turn on your computer and mobile phone, and from then on you don't stop. You're all stressed because you haven't had time to finish putting the presentation together, and by three in the afternoon you still haven't managed to have lunch. Then your boss comes up, looking angry, and asks how the presentation is coming along. How do you think you'll be likely to react? Mechanically, impulsively, without any control over your attitude or behaviour? Or will you be able to respond calmly, assertively, confidently and consciously?"

Emmanuelle and Alice gave each other a conspiratorial glance.

"If your process of self-knowledge and personal development has made you truly coherent and conscious, then you'll inevitably start to change some of your daily habits," continued Paul. "You'll need to develop a healthy, sustainable lifestyle, where you balance work and rest, physical activity and mental relaxation. That's why socially responsible companies are gradually encouraging policies that will allow employees to reconcile their personal and family lives with their work.

'As I said, consciousness is the space we create between what happens to us and our reactions or responses to it. The less vital energy we have, the less conscious and more reactive we are. Which means we need to identify the things that deplete our energy, and the things that give us more of it. Western science has empirically proved that the greatest drain on our energy is negative thinking. And just think of how debilitating arguments and anger are, how empty they leave us! Practising positive thinking, though, will replenish your energy reserves. The best way to generate energy is to have a good time with other people, anywhere at all, in any situation."

"What about you, Paul? What do you do to raise your energy level and get in touch with your essence?" asked Emmanuelle.

"Personally, I've found out that exercising during the day is really good for me; I try to eat high-energy foods, and think positively. I also spend some time each day meditating."

"Meditating?" repeated Bernard.

"I mean, learning to connect with my inner self and anchor myself in the present. I find it's great to go to a park, sit down on a bench and just do nothing except breathe and relax. And one thing that really fills me with energy is watching kids play. It makes me feel closer to the child inside me... It is hard to just do nothing, though. At first, I remember it made me feel really uncomfortable, because it connected me to all my anxiety, to all the pain I'd accumulated in the past... Bit by bit, though, after hours sitting there, breathing and relaxing, I connected to a deep inner peace that made me feel united with everything around me. Meditating, for me, is living in the present. And that's something you can do alone, when you're in the dark, somewhere silent, - or when you're washing the dishes, say. When you learn to use your mind as you wish, consciously, it's much easier to manage your self, and also to respond to life more effectively. And when you stop wasting energy, you learn to make more of it inside you, and you enter into a virtuous circle. You can only be conscious when you're feeling energetic. And only when you're conscious can you practise the art of wisdom.

'When you start managing your self more consciously, cultivating your vital energy, then you move into the third phase of the wonderful process of personal development. After information and energy comes training. And that's what we're going to be doing from now on in this organisation. George is strongly committed to giving you the best possible working conditions, but all I'd ask you to do is to think of the Machine Room as an amazing school, where you'll be able to train at not reacting egocentrically, and in responding more consciously to your daily challenges and problems. Actually, if you wouldn't mind, George , I'd like to rename the Machine Room and call it the Learning Room."

"Fine – let's call it that," agreed the chairman.

THE ART OF COMPASSION

"What I'm going to suggest now might seem totally preposterous," said Paul; "but I'd like to ask you to consider your boss, Ian Insley, as your greatest teacher in personal growth."

This was greeted with incredulous stares.

George Lovejoy, though, had something to say. "We all know Ian hasn't been himself for the past few months. I did have some idea of this before, but now I realise exactly how much he's been suffering. It's made him a slave to his ego, don't you see?

That's why he's so reactive and ill-tempered the whole time... But what do you think we can do about it, Paul?"

"The best thing each one of you can do for Ian is to be at peace with yourselves. If you manage that, it'll stop you from reacting mechanically in your interactions with him, and enable you to change your attitudes into something more beneficial on both sides. Also, if you want him to change at all, the most effective way of bringing this about is to accept him as he is. Accepting doesn't mean agreeing with the way he speaks or does things. Nor does it mean resigning yourselves, or tolerating him. It just means stopping your impulsive reactions and replacing them with a more conscious, loving, constructive response. If each one of us managed to accept him as he is, Ian would stop wasting his time and energy fighting against us, and get closer to realising he's the co-creator of his problems and conflicts and has a responsibility for them. If he comes across no external resistance, he'll eventually have to confront himself and look in the mirror.

'Also, as Ian is a part of this company," Paul went on with a peculiar sparkle in his eyes, "so I'm going to ask you to be compassionate with him. And please don't think that means feeling sorry for him or anything like that. True compassion consists in understanding that someone is suffering, and realising that suffering goes hand in hand with negative attitudes and behaviour. It will also make you realise that Ian isn't actually in charge of himself. He doesn't want to shout or get angry, or be in a bad mood all the time. Nobody wants to live like that, do they? The problem is simply that he's being enslaved by his ego, by his emotional survival mechanisms... It might not seem like it, but he's behaving as well as he can within his own level of comprehension, his level of consciousness and, particularly, how he feels - mainly, sad and dissatisfied. Blame and evil don't actually exist. What does exist in great abundance is ignorance and unconsciousness, which end up inflating people's egos so heavily they'll end up doing anything to hurt others. Ian is going through a process of his own, like all of us. As I said, people often need to hit rock bottom before they'll change. He'll probably go on behaving exactly the same way until something happens to saturate him. I know it isn't easy, but I trust that your love and acceptance will finally inspire him to find the path into himself."

Paul was moving into the most practical part of the course, but before he went ahead with it, he opened his rucksack and gave everyone present a copy of an introductory book on self-knowledge and personal development.

"This book is one of my favourites," he said. "Some time ago, it made me see I knew nothing about life or myself. I still often re-read it, because I want to keep reminding myself of how important it is to be humble and honest with yourself. Think of it as your notes from the course. As I've said, if you want any of this information to make any difference in your lives, you'll need to re-read and repeat it time and time again. Only then will you be able to reprogram your minds voluntarily and consciously. Anyway, I hope you find this book as inspirational as I did. Reading it made me rediscover life. It changed me forever."

VIII
SEARCHING FOR YOURSELF

Monday 10th June 2003

    Several months had gone by since flexitime had been introduced at SAT as a part of George's efforts to improve his staff's working conditions. Each employee had been provided with a laptop and mobile phone so that they could communicate virtually with their clients from wherever they chose, and wouldn't need to go by the office every day. The only exception was Linda Orizio. Being the receptionist required her presence at the office. In return her salary was raised, though her job was just the same as ever. This new policy of abundance and generosity was put forward and encouraged by Lovejoy himself.

    Management by objectives was also introduced. This gave workers an exact idea of what they were asked to accomplish each month. It also gave them greater independence and helped them organise their time more freely, easily reconciling their personal and working lives. A leader was appointed in each department to supervise and coordinate the new trusting arrangement, and he or she had to report to Ian Insley on the first Monday of each month.

    These new flexible policies were all suggested by Paul Prince, greeted with approval by George Lovejoy, eagerly accepted by the staff, and reacted to in anger by Ian Insley. His bad temper was becoming truly unsustainable.

    "Damn that Little Prince!" he shouted at George Lovejoy. "Acting like we can trust all of them like that! It'll bring the company to its knees, you'll see! What this company needs is control, not trust. Why can't you back me on this! If I have no idea where my staff are then how am I supposed to know what they're up to? If I can't tell them what to do, what kind of job can I do as their boss? Am I the only one who hasn't gone stark raving mad here? I don't understand why you can't see that all this policy will do is make us completely lose control of our staff! You should never forget that people will only respect what they fear!"

    But George stood firm on his principles and took no notice of Ian's complaints. He was trusting in what he couldn't see, and beginning to feel it, and listening to what his heart told him, ignoring his doubts, fears and insecurities. For the first time ever, he believed in something: he knew that sooner or later he would manage to make the company he'd set up twenty years before a more human place.

    The radical change in his values was beginning to influence the rest of his life, too. He was enjoying his work more and more, but he still managed to spend more time with his family. His wife found it hard to believe that the sweet, loving executive who came home to her was the man she'd married. A stranger who called himself 'Dad' started calling up and paying visits on his children. And they saw that George wasn't the stressed-out, hurried man he had been, and that he was sincerely interested in them and their lives...

At SAT, meanwhile, the staff had decided to put up a list on the Learning Room wall of some of the main conclusions of Paul's introductory course on self-knowledge and personal development. *Learning at work,* read the framed text, and it continued with ten sentences.

1. Health, satisfaction, well-being and happiness are the natural state of our lives. Illness, dissatisfaction, unhappiness and suffering are unnatural.
2. In between an external stimulus and the way we react to it internally is a space where we have the freedom to choose the most convenient response.
3. When we feel fear, anger and sadness, it means that we have interpreted things egocentrically and thus subjectively, falsely and erroneously.
4. Being a slave to our emotional reactions makes us slaves to our circumstances.
5. When we have little vital energy we become less conscious and more reactive. The more energy we accumulate, the more conscious we become and the easier it is to choose the way we respond.
6. Everyone does the best they can, so we should learn to accept others as they are and flow with the course of things.
7. Blame and evil do not exist. What does exist is ignorance, not knowing who we are, and the unconsciousness of not wanting to know.
8. Complaining and getting angry won't change what has happened. It will destroy our inner well-being.
9. Believing ourselves to be victims of others and of circumstance is the problem. The solution lies in understanding that we are the only ones responsible for our well-being or unhappiness.
10. Success is not the foundation of happiness. Happiness is the foundation of sustainable, meaningful success.

Paul walked into SAT one day, and there was Bernard sweeping the floor, humming something he intended to be a song.

"Morning, Paul. How was your weekend?"

"Morning Bernard," said Paul, heading towards the stairs, his rucksack on his back. "Bit busy today... Mind if we talk some other time? Have a nice day, won't you?" and he ran up the stairs.

Bernard frowned and scratched his chin. "Why couldn't he just stop for a quick chat?" he wondered. But then, he put a stop to his mechanical train of thought. Bernard Martin had just realised that instead of simply accepting what had just happened, he was complaining reactively about what hadn't occurred. "My well-being depends on me and only me," he thought. Chuckling, he went on sweeping.

Paul went into the reception, then sat down and put down his rucksack beside him. He was feeling a bit edgy, and decided to stop and breathe quietly for a moment. As he did so he could hear Linda Orizio talking to someone on the phone.

"Look, I completely understand, but I'm afraid I just can't put you through to him right now," she was saying. "Mr. Lovejoy isn't in his office, and he's asked me not to redirect any calls to his mobile phone."

A top executive from one of the firm's most important client companies was demanding she put him through to the chairman immediately. She could tell from his tone of voice that he was extremely stressed. It was, like always, an urgent matter. Linda carried on talking respectfully to him, but he started yelling at her, saying she didn't know who she was talking to.

Linda nearly let her reactivity get the better of her, but finally she smiled and said to herself, "How funny! This guy isn't shouting at me; he's shouting at his telephone!" Then she held the receiver away from her ear. "Don't take it personally, Linda," she thought. "He must be having a bad day, and he's quite within his rights to get angry because he can't talk to George . Anyway, he won't stop me from being happy, will he..." She took a deep breath and then put the receiver to her ear again.

"Excuse me, sir. I'm really sorry I can't put you through to Mr. Lovejoy. If you don't mind, I'll tell him to call you urgently as soon as he gets into the office. Would you be so kind as to give me your name and telephone number, please?"

The executive berated her for a while longer, but finally gave her his number. When she'd hung up, Linda gave Paul a grateful smile. "What I give to others is the only thing I have at the end of the day," she whispered to herself. "My self-esteem depends on me and me only, on the way I see myself and behave towards myself."

Paul was feeling more relaxed. He got up, picked up his rucksack, and wordlessly kissed Linda on both cheeks. She went bright red.

"You're looking good today," he said.

"Thanks, Paul. You're not looking too bad yourself."

And Paul also blushed.

"Well, you know what the mystics say..." he said.

"No – what is it?"

"Beauty is in the eye of the beholder."

Linda smiled and put her hand over her mouth. "Those mystics!" she said, touching her hair. "Do they do anything else apart from all their experiments and philosophising? I mean, do they ever eat?"

"Sure they do! The real mystics don't even fast – they see life as a huge banquet!" Paul laughed.

"Thank god," said Linda.

Neither of them said anything for a brief while. Then Linda spoke up.

"Paul, how about inviting me to dinner tonight? There's this restaurant..."

"Sorry, restaurants aren't really my thing," he said.

"Oh. I just thought that..."

"...but if you like, I'd love you to come round to my place and I'll make you something nice."

Linda's face lit up. Her heart started beating so hard she almost felt like Paul might hear it.

"Great!" she said enthusiastically.

"Wonderful. See you tonight, then."

And Linda nodded.

"Anyway, now that that's sorted out, could you tell me where George is?" asked Paul.

"He's with his family – he asked me not to bother him on any account."

Suddenly, the phone rang. It was the secretary of the businessman she'd been speaking to before. She was calling to apologise on his behalf.

Linda thanked the woman for the unexpected gesture of good will, while Paul headed to the Learning Room. He had an urgent matter to see to. He was wanting to speak to Alice Osaka. It was eleven in the morning and the place was nearly empty, with just a couple of people in each department. To date, the firm was not only continuing to function; it was doing so more profitably and productively. Paul Prince had even written up a series of questionnaires for their clients to find out how satisfied they were with the way SAT was working. For the first time ever, the Learning Room was a calm, pleasant place to be.

Paul apologised to Alice for being late and then put his rucksack down on her desk.

"Don't worry," she said with a shrug.

"How are you feeling today?"

"Fine, as always," she replied, looking away. "How about you?" She folded her arms over the bulge in her belly.

"I called you in today because I was wanting to talk to you about your pregnancy."

"My what? I don't know what you mean, Paul."

"How many months pregnant are you, Alice?"

"I know I've put on a few kilos, but..."

But Paul Prince never gave up on a question. "Alice," he insisted, looking straight into her eyes, "how many months pregnant are you?"

Alice hugged her belly and stared at the ground.

"I said, I'm not pregnant. Thanks for being so concerned, but please just let me be." Tears welled in the corner of her eyes.

Paul hugged her.

"I don't want to lose my job," she sniffed.

"You won't, don't worry," Paul whispered into her ear. "I know SAT has made some unfortunate decisions in the past, but things have changed now."

"I never said anything to you because I was afraid of being the fifth pregnant woman to be fired in the last four years."

"I know, I understand. But I promise, you're going to be the first one to stay on, and you'll be an example for other women of how they can work and be a mother at the same time. We'll start doing the paperwork this afternoon for your maternity leave. How can anyone work for a place that won't let its staff pursue their most important interests? Being a mother is the greatest journey you can ever make! Children can teach us everything we need to know! You'll see, you're going to have all the support you need from the company, because that's what you deserve. It'll all be fine, I promise."

Alice took out her handkerchief and smiled. Then, looking directly at Paul, she said, "But Paul, what are we going to do about Ian?"

"Forget about him. It looks like from now on, Ian is going to have to watch over himself rather than others."

For some reason Alice didn't quite understand, they both laughed.

At the other end of the Learning Room, Emmanuelle Evans was deeply engrossed in the presentation she was putting together. She took a brief moment's pause and crossed her hands behind her head, leaning back in her chair. "Things really are changing here," she thought. Meanwhile, Ian Insley was going over another report that she'd handed in a couple of days back. He was alone in a cloud of smoke inside his office. His ashtray was crowded with the morning's ten cigarettes. He read through the report and gave a heavy sigh.

"Christ, Emmanuelle!" he mentally rebuked her. "Is this what you call doing your job? Lucky for you you're not the only incompetent one here... All of them have let me down, really. They just don't care. Even George betrayed me with that naivety of his. That Little Prince he loves so much, I don't know what they all see in him, damn him. I don't know what else I can do to get things back to normal."

He looked down at the ring on his finger and slumped a little in his chair. Thinking of his wife made him realise he was vulnerable, and also that he'd been in pain for months and it wasn't going away.

"Now, Ian, don't start. Breathe, go on." He inhaled and exhaled deeply. "Come on, you need to go and speak to Emmanuelle and tell her what you think, alright? But careful, no shouting today. Just remember, not everyone is able to take their work so seriously or do such a good job as you. You have to show them you're a human being just like them, now..."

After this little speech to himself, Ian Insley gently opened his office door. A dense cloud of smoke flowed out of it, and in the distance he heard Emmanuelle Evans giggle.

Alice and Paul were chatting about something, he could see. Ian threw his cigarette butt on the ground and crushed it under his heel, then went down the spiral staircase to Emmanuelle's cubicle.

"Morning, Emmanuelle. How are you today?"

She stared at him in surprise.

"Um, fine, I guess."

"Good. Anyway, I've just been reading through your report, and I have to say I'm not all that happy with it." Ian was trying hard to be polite.

"Oh! Um, I don't know... I really tried to do a good job. It took me six weeks to do," said Emmanuelle, whose right leg was starting to twitch under her desk.

"Yes, yes... I'm sure you tried." Ian was losing control. "But I'm afraid you're going to have to redo it. Just look at the colour of the front page – it's awful! And I found at least three spelling mistakes. Now, please look through all my corrections and get working on it. And have it finished before you leave." He dropped the report on her desk.

Ian was annoyed at himself for having been so rude. But realising this just made him even more angry. Emmanuelle Evans, meanwhile, was asking herself, "What is it you find so hard to accept, Emmanuelle? Ian isn't finding fault with you, but with the report. And that's only because he's really unhappy with himself, so he can't see things objectively."

Emmanuelle paged through her report. Every single page had red marks on it. She'd have to redo it completely.

"There are sixty-two pages here. I really don't know if I'll have time to do the whole thing today," she said tentatively.

That was too much for Ian.

"I don't care if there are five hundred or eight thousand pages. We don't leave our work half-done here! This is a serious company, don't you get it?"

"Nobody can hurt you unless you let them," Emmanuelle reminded herself. "Nothing he can say is going to make you react. Your confidence depends on you. Accept Ian; right now he doesn't know what he's doing, or have any idea he could do it better."

"I'm sorry, Ian. I'll change the front page and work on the spelling, and I'll redo it all as you say," she replied, keeping calm.

Insley was huffing and puffing like an angry bull.

"Right, that's what I want, Emmanuelle... now, remember, the most important thing in life is to take things seriously, to do a good job." He was trying hard to contain himself.

Emmanuelle was feeling like she'd just managed some kind of epic feat. "Well done, girl!" she congratulated herself. Ian was still frowning and shaking his head in front of her. He took a quick look around the Learning Room, saw how empty it was, then shouted, "Where the hell is everyone!"

No answer was forthcoming. Stalking out of Emmanuelle's cubicle, Insley came face to face with the list on the wall. And that was the last straw. He ripped it off and strode over to Paul, enraged.

"This is all your damn fault, Paul!" he yelled. "I'm sick of all this crap, all your armchair psychology and dumb values! I don't want to see your stupid smile a second longer!"

He threw the list on the ground as hard as he could. The wooden frame and glass front shattered into smithereens. Ian suddenly slumped his shoulders. The air seemed to go out of him. The staff stood around him, amazed.

"All of you! What are you staring at?" he turned on them.

Ian's eyes were swollen, red and glistening. They looked like two balloons about to burst. But before his tears would give him away, he ran into his office, slamming the door behind him in true style. Alone in there, he collapsed onto his desk, weeping. "I can't go on like this, I need help. I can't bear myself any longer! I can't go on living like this! What have I turned into?"

Ian stayed inside his office for some time. Meanwhile, in the Learning Room, Paul focused his efforts on calming down the rest of the staff. It wasn't hard, in spite of the strength of Insley's outburst. His behaviour had spoken so loud there was no need for words. For the first time, the group felt truly sympathetic towards their boss. Nobody dared pass judgement on him. Emmanuelle Evans, Alice Osaka, Linda Orizio and all the rest understood that Ian simply couldn't control what he said or the way he behaved. Even since he'd come back to work after his month off, their boss had been in the grip of something dark. He'd become a slave to his own unhappiness, and also the master of it.

Only Paul knew the real cause of his suffering. That morning, he'd met up for breakfast with Ian's wife. She'd spent two whole hours telling him what the couple were going through.

That afternoon after his family lunch, George Lovejoy met up with Paul Prince in his office to address the issue of Ian. Paul went in, put down his rucksack and sat down next to the chairman.

"I heard what happened with Ian," said George, shaking his head sadly. "We all know how impulsive and bad-tempered he is. But he's gone too far this time. I feel really bad, because I love him like he was my own son. Plus he's the most experienced worker here. If it weren't for his attitude... I was planning a raise for him, but it looks like he's just not willing to change. I don't know, Paul – I'm beginning to consider dismissing him. It might be the best thing for the company," he said uncertainly.

"You won't need to do that, George ."

"Why not?"

"Well, dismissing Ian would only make him more resentful towards us and about life. I had a talk with his wife this morning – she's a lovely person, by the way... Anyway, I know what the matter is with him. Remember the month he took off?"

"Yes. It was the first time in three years he'd been off work for more than a month. And I don't even know any more whether that's something to praise or complain about!"

"Ian's wife," continued Paul, "told me that the reason for that was that Ian found out that he's sterile. Having children was what he wanted more than anything in the world. Who would have thought he was dying to be a father?"

George was dumbstruck.

"His wife asked if we'd be patient and try to help him out," said Paul. "And that's what I'd suggest we do."

Lovejoy nodded.

"Count on me."

"Actually, I also think Ian is a really worthy man, and we're going to need him here to build the future we want... The only thing that's wrong is that he's been addicted to his bad moods, his negativity and victimisation for too long. But all of those illnesses can be cured, luckily. I think that what he needs most is to get back in touch with reality. And to do that, he needs to experience something that will connect him with his inner self again."

"Go on."

"If we really want the best for him, we have to give him the chance to sort out his problems for himself. What I'd suggest is that the company pay for a trip in July and August, and consider it as training for him."

"Pay for a trip?" exclaimed George. He paused, then sighed. "Okay then. We'll do it. That was my ego speaking just then. The little guy really comes to the forefront when money has anything to do with it!"

Paul laughed with him. "George, I think we need to help Ian win the greatest struggle of all: conquering himself."

"And how do you think he should go about that?"

"Travelling around Madagascar on his own."

The chairman raised his eyebrows in surprise, but then nodded to disguise it.

"I don't know if you're aware of this, George – but travelling on your own is a wonderful way to combat unhappiness."

"I'm sure you're right, but isn't Madagascar a bit far away? What's Ian going to find there?"

"Hopefully, he'll find himself... Madagascar is a remote island, a true paradise where the environment still rules over the tarmac. Most people live right in nature! To help Ian out, I've packed his rucksack for him. I put in a first aid kit, a map, the book on self-knowledge I gave you all, and a list of people he might come across during his journey."

"His journey? What do you mean?"

"If he agrees to the adventure, Ian will make a thousand kilometre journey. And he'll walk all the way, with only his passport, rucksack and shadow for company. I'll suggest a route for him that goes from Fort Dauphin in the south east to the capital, Antananarivo."

"How come you know so much about Madagascar?"

"Because that's where I went travelling before I came here. I have no doubt it'll be the worst, and the best experience he'll ever have."

George thought for a while, trying to imagine how Ian would react to the idea.

"It's crazy," he said. "But desperate situations need desperate solutions, right?"

"His wife thinks it's a good idea. And his rucksack is packed. I just asked Linda to book his ticket for the first of June. So, if you agree to it, all we need is his consent."

"I trust you, Paul. And I trust this journey will do wonders for Ian. I'm going to call his wife up now. I haven't spoken to her for ages..."

"Actually, you're expected at dinner at their place tonight."

George stared at Paul wide-eyed. And Paul opened his rucksack and pulled out a bottle of red wine, handing it to his boss with a smile.

"Here. Something tells me you're going to need this."

"I really hit the jackpot with you, didn't I."

"Thanks. I'm delighted to be your Personal and Corporate Values Manager."

"Are you sure you never did an MBA?"

"No – I told you, they're horribly expensive, and they still..."

"I know, I know... they still don't teach any of the things that really matter."

IX

CAREFUL!
POWER ISOLATES AND CORRUPTS

Thursday 1st July 1999

At the consulting firm where Paul Prince had worked when he was twenty-seven, the senior partners' office was on the top floor of the building. Those who worked there were known among the rest of the staff as 'the guys upstairs'. Sitting in one of the glass-walled offices which looked out over the city were the long-standing Human Resources Manager, and Paul's immediate boss. He was smoking a cigar and trying to wind down after an intense day's work, and sharing his view of the small world inside the large company.

"Isn't it great when things go well?" he said. "How about we open a bottle of whisky?"

"Yeah, make it strong, will you?" replied Paul's boss, rubbing his neck.

The manager rolled his comfortable office chair over to the minibar and generously filled two finely-cut tumblers.

"Any problem with 'the guys downstairs'?" he asked, puffing out a large mouthful of smoke.

"Take a guess. Bunch of lazy bastards. The only problem with this place is the incompetence of the staff. Why do the guys downstairs find it so hard to follow our way of doing things? If we're number one in the market it must be for a good reason, right?"

The human resources manager nodded and handed Paul's boss a tumbler. The man took a sip. "I don't know what they teach those boys at university and business school, but I get the feeling they're growing dumber and dumber. They never think for themselves; all they do is obey, obey. And they work so slowly and don't do a good job."

"Don't be so drastic, man." The human resources manager smiled slyly and the wrinkles on his face stood out. "Remember, most of those boys don't have any idea who they are or what they're doing here. They're all stiff with fear. They're so scared to move that not one of them ever dares complain about how they're being exploited. I'm the human resources manager, I should know!"

The two men laughed and clinked their glasses. After the toast, the veteran manager went on.

"They're scared of life and its uncertainties. And that means we have a lot of docile, easily manageable people under us. That'll never work against us, see? Otherwise why would we call them 'useful idiots'? You're right, they have no initiative, but we shouldn't complain about that. They're cheap, aren't they? They give us their lives for a pittance of a salary and a false feeling of security."

"You're totally right," admitted Paul's boss, taking a deep, satisfying puff on his cigar. "Sorry, I'm just a bit more stressed than normal right now. I haven't slept for three months. And I wake up in a real bad mood... I don't know, I guess I'll get over it. I haven't been feeling that great ever since my wife divorced me, and..."

"Have another whisky," said the human resources manager.

"Erm, sure, why not? Anyway, as I was saying, my wife left me last year, and I'm finding it hard..."

"Never mind, things will get better soon." The other man cut him off, sliding the glass of whisky over to him.

An uncomfortable silence followed.

"By the way," said the human resources manager, "how are things going with that young smartass you told me about?"

"Who? Prince?" said Paul's boss, still staring at the ground.

"Yeah, him, the Little Prince."

"I'd rather you hadn't mentioned him, actually. He just does his own thing. He won't let anyone exploit him... Guess what he told me the other day? He said there were too many big shots here and not enough human values. Can you believe it?"

The human resources manager lit his cigar again. "I've been around too long for anything to surprise me, I tell you. I do find it funny, though, that someone could be naïve enough to complain about the lack of... what did you say he called it?"

"Human values."

The manager burst out laughing, dropping ash from his cigar on his tie.

"So, the Little Prince says there are no human values here, does he?" he echoed his colleague, frowning. "What are values anyway? Where does that runt think he works? Does he think we're here to run round like some kind of NGO, a bunch of nuns or something?"

The human resources manager got up and paced around his desk.

"Look, I'm in a good mood today, so I'm going to help you solve your problems with that guy. I'm gonna give him a lesson he'll never forget, you'll see. Send for him, will you? I'll soon get rid of his pathetic naivety."

Paul's boss went out of the office and made a phonecall. Inside, the human resources manager stared into the empty space of his office.

"What does that pipsqueak think? Does he think I haven't realised how cruel and corrupt this system is? That the huge corporations are the cancer of this world?" he thought. "I'm not some kind of idiot, am I. What he doesn't know is that as long as my salary comes in every month I don't give a damn about anything else!"

His colleague came back in, and they sat across the desk from each other with their whiskies, waiting for Paul Prince to come in. The human resources manager's secretary called to say that Paul was waiting.

"Tell him we'll be ready in ten minutes," ordered the man. "That's how long they need to figure out who's boss," he joked to Paul's boss.

Ten minutes later, Paul walked firmly into the office.

"Morning, Mr. Prince. Please take a seat. I asked you to come up because we wanted you to join our little celebration."

"Call me Paul, will you? Mr. Prince is my father."

"As you wish. Now, let me get straight to the point. We've been hearing some... complaints about you. Apparently you're somewhat of a... rebel. Some people say you tend to do whatever you want, and that you refuse to adapt to the needs of the company."

"Well, I guess I don't think it's such an intelligent attitude to adapt to such an... inhuman, toxic environment," Paul answered, mimicking the manager's tone of voice.

He turned his head towards his boss and added, "As I often say, I don't believe in what I do, because this firm has no values. And work has no meaning to me without values. You know better than I do how easy it is to earn money. The difficult thing is to respect others while you do it, generating real wealth for society and respecting our environment. Wouldn't you agree?"

The human resources manager smiled. He was trying to mask the anger welling up inside him. "Is he trying to take the piss out of me?" he wondered. "Let me show this guy how things work in the real world. He thinks he knows himself, does he? Everyone has a price, though. And now we're going to find out his..."

Out loud, he said, "Totally, totally. It isn't easy, though... And that's why we need you here, in this firm. We want to make it a more human place, you see, and we need your help," he lied. "Your boss and I were just talking about it. We know you're worth a lot, Paul. And we want to bring you up a couple of steps in the organisation. We've just decided to raise you to senior consultant. That means you'll have more responsibilities, and have a team of six working under you. And, of course, you'll earn a better salary... You're only going to be five floors under us from now on. And if you stick at it and learn to make some sacrifices, in a few years time you might just become a partner in the firm. How do you feel about that, now?"

Paul looked straight at him. With a small smile, he said, "No thanks. I'm leaving here today. This company is meaningless, and I'm quite sure that it's going to go under just because of the way it's run."

"What!" The human resources manager was outraged. His eyes were red. "You mean you're just going to throw away what I'm giving you, just like that?"

"If that's what you call success," answered Paul calmly, "then I'd prefer to be a failure."

"But what the hell will you do out there? There's so much competition in the market!" the manager insisted.

"I really have no idea. The only thing I know is that I don't want to be here any more. It's more serious for me to 'try to understand why flowers go to such trouble to produce thorns that are good for nothing.' That seems far more interesting to me than adding and subtracting all day as if I were an important man like you..."

Paul got up and held out his hand to the manager, who shook it reluctantly, not really understanding what he'd just heard. Next to him, Paul's boss gave a brief goodbye nod. Paul marched out of the office, his heart brimming with self-confidence, and a new chapter in his life began. Unlike the chapters before it, this one would be written in his own hand.

And just three weeks later, he left to travel the world with all the money he'd saved since he'd started working at the firm. He was quite sure about it: there was no way he'd be back until he'd found out who he was, what he was good at, and the meaning he wanted to give his life. It would take him three years, one month and eleven days to do so.

X

**MATURITY COMES WITH REALISING
YOU'RE NOT A VICTIM OF YOUR CIRCUMSTANCES**

Monday 1st September 2003

Emmanuelle Evans couldn't remember the last time she'd been glad it was Monday. She stopped to take a look in the mirror just before she left for work. She was happy to be starting again. She stared at herself. She was feeling slightly strange and confused. She even wondered at her own enthusiasm.

"What's up with you today, Emmanuelle?" she thought. "Why are you feeling so happy?"

In actual fact, she was finding it hard to relate her good mood to the job she was going to be doing from then on at SAT. After a working life pitted with frustration and frustration, Emmanuelle was finally glimpsing the chance to have a useful, creative, meaningful career. Paul Prince had recommended to Lovejoy that she be raised. She was the new Director of Personal Growth Training. Her job was to research into available tools for self-knowledge and personal growth for leadership based on values and organisational change. Months ago, she would have felt uncertain about it. But Emmanuelle was no longer afraid. She trusted in her ability to give the best of herself. She'd have to begin by learning and growing as much as she could, but in the mid-term she'd have the task of organising special courses for the company's clients. The mere thought of it made her heart fill with joy.

Emmanuelle's rise wasn't the only change at SAT. Seven out of its thirty-eight employees left the company when their summer holidays began. Encouraged by Paul and the company, they'd decided to make a turnaround in their own lives and move into more vocational professions.

"I'd invite you to keep on searching inside yourselves to find out who you really are, what you like, what makes you buzz; what it is you're really after in life. That's the only way for you to really know how you can work towards making things around you better. And if what you want is to be happy at work, remember it's not what you receive that matters, but what you give... Never forget that true success lies in loving what you do and doing what you love, thinking of your work with a will to serve. If you manage that, then everything else will come along with it."

Ian Insley was travelling around Madagascar. George Lovejoy' and his wife's suggestion had come as a shock at first; but after a while he realised it might not be a bad idea to leave for a while and face the deep unhappiness that had rooted in his mind and heart. Nobody at the company knew exactly where he was. But he sent his wife postcards every week telling her how much he missed her. He was following Paul's route.

Alice Osaka was on maternity leave. She'd just given birth to a baby boy called Luke. Being a mother was turning out to be the most incredible experience she'd ever had. Or at least that was what she told Paul when he went to see her at the hospital.

Meanwhile, George Lovejoy had been taking on new workers. In selecting them, he no longer focused exclusively on their professional trajectories or experience. Along with the necessary technical expertise, what he sought was emotionally healthy people with well-trained positive attitudes. Lovejoy knew what he wanted. Working for SAT required values such as responsibility, humility, genuineness, trust, courage, enthusiasm, and a real capacity for teamwork. More than skilled professionals, what he needed were human beings in touch with themselves and others, conscious and committed to developing their own potential.

"I'm looking for people who enjoy the mystery of a magical life," he admitted to Paul one day.

The last, but not the least important of the changes at SAT took Emmanuelle by surprise on the morning she went back to work after her August break. She turned on the lights and saw that there had been nothing less than a revolution in the Learning Room. Following a recommendation by Paul, George Lovejoy had hired the services of a firm specialised in redesigning working environments. Nobody knew exactly how, but in the space of a month they'd managed to provide the room with natural light and healthy ventilation. The walls were painted yellow, orange, pink and red. The cubicles were gone, and the Learning Room was now an open space where each member of staff had his or her own table and could communicate with the rest without picking up the phone.

The room was filled with plants and creepers. Nature was present too. The new space breathed life. Five minutes after she walked in, Emmanuelle was still gaping in surprise. And her eyes nearly popped out when she saw that one of the corners had been turned into a chill-out space for resting, reading and relaxing. The space was exclusively for SAT staff, and there were books there on personal growth, organisational change, and other financial and business topics. Emmanuelle sat down on one of the sofas and put her feet up on a pouf. She folded her hands behind her neck and smiled. A few metres away was a huge transparent fridge filled with yoghurts, fruit and juices.

Ian's was the only office space still standing. It no longer had a door, only a glass wall onto the Learning Room. Emmanuelle smiled again. Everyone would be able to see Ian from down below. Much as she hated to admit it, the space had been flawlessly designed to create a good working environment. Their new working conditions left no room for complaints or anyone playing the victim. From then on, responsibility for the staff's well-being and productivity lay entirely on themselves, and would depend solely on their ability to effectively relate to themselves and others.

One by one, all the staff came trickling in. Like Emmanuelle, they all had to pinch themselves to make sure they weren't dreaming. After months of deep inner change set off by the introductory course on self-knowledge and personal development, the time had finally come for them to be rewarded with an important outward transformation: a change in their work space. More than one of them even seriously joked about exchanging the office for their home to work at. However they chose to do it, though, they'd have the freedom to do their work wherever they pleased.

While the typical round of post-vacational hugs and greetings was going on, George Lovejoy saw that over the past few months, members of the different departments were much more friendly towards each other. consultants chatted with marketing employees, marketing with IT, IT with finance, finance with consultants. "What are we doing here!" thought Lovejoy. "If I ever tried to tell it, no-one would believe me!"

All the staff sat down and Lovejoy asked for a moment of silence.

"Hello to everyone, and welcome to the new SAT!" he announced. "As you know, we've spent the last year trying to improve your working conditions in the hope that it'll help you give us the best of yourselves. Our new commitment is to get this company's systems and technology to work for people, above all. I'm mentioning this because I recently realised something terribly obvious: that the personal dimension is far more important than the professional dimension. And that by taking care of people, you help them do their jobs..."

Just then, the door opened and in came Paul Prince. He stood at the back of the Learning Room to watch George.

"I just want to thank you all for your support, enthusiasm and patience," the chairman went on. "As you know, it took me nearly sixty years to get this project running in a way that I found meaningful and humane on both a personal and professional level. But now that I've finally come to my senses, all I want is that all of us together can begin a period in our lives which will be full of challenges and enjoyment – that's what we're here for, after all! And to celebrate the first day of the rest of our lives as individuals and as the SAT team, I want to read you a very special letter... It's from Ian, and it's addressed to all of us. He asked me to read it to all of you. He's coming back this afternoon and will be here later."

The announcement caused a stir of unease. Whispers went round. George looked around for Paul and waved to greet him. The entire staff watched as the chairman opened up an envelope and took out two handwritten pages.

"'Dear friends and colleagues,'" he read. "'I know this letter is the last thing you will have expected to receive. It's not a postcard. I'm not wanting to send you my holiday news. It's a confession. It contains no sarcastic comments, no insults, no lack of respect or anything of the sort. So please just sit back, relax and listen.

"The first thing I'd like to say is that I'm sorry. I'd like to say sorry to each one of you for the way I've behaved ever since I was made chief consultant; particularly over the last twelve months. I'm not intending this letter to be some kind of justification for what I did, and nor do I want to make excuses. I only want to admit to the mistakes I made, and to take responsibility for what I did and do.

'Surprising as it may seem, this is me: Ian. Your despotic, bad-tempered boss, the man who made your life a misery at work. Something inside me has changed. And I think it's changed forever. I still can't quite believe it's me writing this letter... But somehow, I just have to do it. This journey I'm on has made a huge impact on me, much bigger than I ever could have imagined. Luckily for all of you, for my wife and for me too, I'm a different man to the one who made that horrible scene the last time I was with you. I'm a bit more conscious now. I know I don't deserve it, but I really hope you'll give me a second chance.

"Travelling through a place as different to what I know as Madagascar has really shown me what it means to be humble. My first few days here were really hard. Antananarivo, the capital, is a chaotic maze of dust, poverty and pollution. The air is so dirty it's hard to even breathe. I can't speak Malagasy or French, so the only person I have for company is myself, twenty-four hours a day. Spending so much time alone without talking made me realise that the anger and rage I feel are just my own pain.

"Also, it's winter here, and it's dark by five. I got to my hotel room, sat down, and started crying. It's hard for me to admit, but I collapsed. Suddenly I started remembering how George and my wife had persuaded me that the trip might be good for me. I was too proud to see it at first, and it took me several weeks to accept the idea. But in the end, it's done me a lot of good. I think it's helped me realise that I was fooling myself, and taking my unhappiness out on everyone else.

"You can have no idea of how hard it was to come to terms with all the pain and suffering I was carrying. I still don't know how I managed to keep going and turn up work every day with so much

poison inside me. Hard as it was to see at first, that was precisely the aim of my journey. I realise that I've found it impossible this year to acknowledge that I would never have children. I admit it: I love kids. I don't know why, but one of the few joys in my life has been to spend time with them. Having a family was my greatest project in life. Being a father was my biggest dream. Perhaps because of that, instead of accepting the fact that I'm sterile, I've channelled all my aggression towards my wife and yourselves. I have no words to express my shame. I know that regretting things is no use – the harm has already been done. All I want and hope for now is that you forgive me. I'm still trying to forgive myself, I promise.

"To tell you something of my journey: I've walked seven hundred and fifty-nine kilometres in fifty-five days, crossing the entire east coast from Fort Dauphin to Antananarivo. I had no idea I was capable of such a feat! I've lost seventeen kilos and grown a beard. A few days into the walk, I realised I was doing penitence. I even walked barefoot some of the way. My feet were in such a bad state I couldn't manage to walk all the way to the airport as I'd originally intended... I eventually managed to drag myself to a small rural clinic and get the painful wound on my left foot treated. It had been infected for several days by then.

"Anyway, I may have mistreated my body, but mentally, I feel more strong and healthy than I ever have. Having been alone for such a long time showed me that everything comes down to the way you relate to yourself. That's why travelling alone has turned out to be so therapeutic. I ended up having no choice but to face the things I was most afraid of: my ego, that tiny, massive 'self', so selfish it's been tearing me up inside for years. As you can see, Paul, I've been studying the book I found in my rucksack. I've read it nine times. At first I laughed at it. But after some time, I started to understand the message in it... Thanks so much for your patience and generosity. It was a great present!

"I'd be lying if I didn't tell you I was close to giving up the whole trip several times. On the first leg of it, my destructive way of thinking became impossible for me to bear. My mind felt like a rubbish dump. Often, when I started walking, I was exhausted and in a bad mood, and found it hard to keep going. I couldn't stop feeling sad, anxious and irritated with myself. It was hell. I felt like I was going to die right then and there. And my feet, my calves, my knees, hips, back, shoulders, neck, all ached... I was destroying my own body! Thousands of excuses came to mind to justify giving up. But I forced myself to go on, whatever it took. Because in spite of the pain, I somehow knew that the experience was just what I needed.

"I'd had to hit rock bottom to realise that I had to change; I had no choice. The only 'problem' in my life was myself. I'd spent forty days alone, walking about fifteen kilometres alone with nobody to help me. It had rained solidly for two weeks and I'd been soaked. But that was precisely the moment when something inside me started to change, and it transformed the way I saw reality. For the first time in ages, I felt peace. I don't quite know how to explain it, but it happened in an amazing, unexpected way. Something shifted inside me. I was walking through a storm, and there was thunder and lightning all around me, and suddenly I started weeping with happiness. I'd never seen so much beauty as I did watching the pink and purple sunset over a baobab forest. For the first time ever, I gave thanks for being alive!

"Apart from that unforgettable experience, another thing that really changed me was coming into contact with the villagers in the south east of Madagascar, which is the area which has been least touched by the western colonial influence. The way we would see it, there's 'nothing to do' there, and 'nothing to do it for'. I slept in a different village each day, in the homes of families who put me up for the night. Can you imagine me, Ian, sleeping on the floor of a hut? I would never have thought it possible. But use your imaginations – they're your greatest treasure... Anyway, as I spent more and more time with the villagers, I had to learn to relate to them, although words weren't exactly the way we did it. And day by day, I started paying less and less attention to my own unhappiness and became more and more interested in the way they think.

"Eighty-five percent of the nineteen million people on the island live in an integrated way with nature, in huts made of bamboo, palm fronds and other leaves. Their diet consists in rice, bananas, oranges (which taste of lemon!), and if they're lucky, potatoes, yam, tomatoes, carrots, onions and fish. Nobody dies of starvation here, but the diet is poor and you can see that in the state of their teeth and stringy muscles. There are also small shops in some of the villages which sell packaged foods – often past their expiry date - like biscuits, sweets, crisps, condensed milk, cigarettes, oil, salt, sugar, warm beer, and fortunately for me, bottled water. There are few hospitals, except in the towns, and hardly any medicines available.

"Men tend to work in the fields, while women stay at home and look after the children, who make up more than sixty percent of the population. The kids come running up to you, grab you by the hand and start playing with you... You can't imagine how much I've enjoyed being with them! I hadn't laughed so much for years! Here in Madagascar I realised that I've spent years of my life without laughing, or even smiling. These children have given it all back to me. They've brought me back to life. They've taught me so many games, and I've spent hours making them laugh too. Amazing! When I was with them I remembered I was old enough to be their biological father. But many of them were orphans. That didn't make them stop smiling though, or give up on life. What a great lesson to learn, and to think it was a bunch of kids who taught it to me!

"As I was saying, from a western point of view they're really poor. But poverty in a material sense has led them to develop a kind of wealth based on values, which is hard to find in developed countries. That needs no explaining, I'm sure. I'm a perfect example of the decadence of western society. But here, I started to unlearn everything I knew. I'm deprogramming myself. I feel liberated; I want to rebuild myself as a human being, to remake my life. I want to learn from my mistakes and become a bit more like the Madagascans... I'm quite convinced about this. They're normally quite introverted people, calm, and they seem to live by the motto, 'Live and let live.' Being here and meeting all these amazing people, I've remembered how great and simple it is to feel you can count on yourself, that whatever happens, you'll be there.

'As you can imagine, this trip has shown me how thoroughly ignorant I was. It's been hugely educational. As I write these lines I'm finding it hard to control my emotions. I'm so sorry for everything I put you all through. I'm sorry you had to put up with me at the office. As my wife, whom I owe everything to, told me the other day, the real journey starts when you return. I hope I'll be able to make it all up to you somehow. Forgive me, please. The man you'll see later on today is different to the one who went away. I've changed. And if you'll let me, I'd love us to be able to begin again. We're a team. And as the man who was your boss, I know now that I have a great deal to learn from you all. I want to learn to serve you.

"With my fondest regards and care,

"Ian.'"

With that, George put the letter down. His eyes were glistening.

He wasn't the only one to have been moved. Alice Osaka hugged Emmanuelle, who shed a brief tear. And Linda Orizio did the same to Paul. The rest of the staff said nothing as they mulled over the letter.

At lunchtime that day, Lovejoy invited Paul Prince out.

"Order whatever you feel like, Paul," he said. "We're here to celebrate, so I'm not going to worry about how much I spend!"

"Thanks, George. I'll have a tomato salad."

The chairman frowned, then smiled.

"Salad! Great! It's been years since I last had one! - Two salads, please, and two pork fillets, rare, if you don't mind. Ah! And a bottle of your very best red wine!"

Paul wasn't a teetotaller or a vegetarian, but he didn't drink or eat meat. "Just this once," he thought to himself.

During lunch they talked about how quickly the year had gone by, and came to a couple of conclusions about it. After one or two glasses of wine, George made a confession.

"It's true that I've been successful at my job, that I've had my share of power and found it exciting, and I've earned more money than I can spend... But let me tell you something: the need for recognition, power and money can imprison the soul. It's so easy to corrupt the heart of an ignorant, greedy man! I'm speaking from experience, I promise you."

Paul said nothing but nodded, so George went on. There were things he'd been needing to say for a long time...

"In actual fact," he said, "I never made a deliberate decision to be a businessman. All I did was follow what other people told me to do. But now I know that when you don't know who or what you are you become a slave to your own lack of self-esteem and insecurity. Your lack of confidence makes you do and think the same as others. And if you dare to be different, nobody ever forgives you for it. In western society now, being yourself means being a revolutionary."

George took another sip of wine. "Lately I've been thinking about how the world works... Ever since we're kids our heads are stuffed with lies telling us how to live our lives. We're filled with fear, told what to study so we won't 'go hungry'. We're conditioned to succeed at any cost, to achieve a certain social status, privileges and take on all kinds of responsibilities, to buy a big house, have too cars and a gorgeous woman by our side. And most of all, we're taught to earn money. Lots of money... Success appears to be a whole lot of stereotypes forced on us by society. You're told that the 'temple of happiness' lies at the top of the ladder, and all you have to do is climb up there. But it's a huge lie. I've been there, and it's empty. There's nothing to be had there. Not a trace of happiness!"

George stroked his bald patch absent-mindedly and took another sip of wine. "All my experience has shown me that success, recognition, power and money will only come when you're selfish and ambitious. And that ends up wiping out all your humanity... it tears you away from your essence, and in that kind of distancing from your true self you end up forgetting all the projects and values that are really worth anything. And the most amazing thing of all is that most of us aren't at all happy, because we've been programmed not to be, but very few of us are humble or brave enough to recognise that. It took me fifty-seven years!"

"Well, better late than never," smiled Paul.

"You're right! Life is now. This isn't some kind of trial run. Lying to ourselves and being afraid does strange things to us. I mean, when we won't acknowledge or speak about the emptiness we feel inside. However much we try to convince ourselves or put on a fake persona, pleasure has nothing to do with happiness. Even today's idea of fun is nothing but a form of escape, an evasion, a kind of drug we take to forget our true selves and the meaninglessness of our lives."

Paul was listening carefully.

"I know, I know," laughed George. "I've spent my whole life wearing a blindfold. And the funny thing is, I put it on myself, and I've refused to take it off until now. I had to die to open my eyes! I'm telling you all this, dear Paul, because I'm grateful to you. With you, I've finally understood my greatest truth, and that is that an emotionally stable life is better than an obsessive search for material wealth. At least for me, true success means caring for other peoples' happiness. For the first time in my whole life, I feel like I'm being coherent with my beliefs. Now I understand what it is to live consciously! When you wake up from the dream of your ego, you realise there's no greater failure than setting yourself false aims and achieving them. That's why so many successful people who're really unhappy: they've just done what the system tells them to, and not what their hearts dictate." He drank down the rest of his wine, and then ended off, "There's one thing I know for sure: if you don't learn to be happy within yourself, you're sure to end up feeling like a failure."

Bernard Martin was cleaning the windows in the hall when Ian Insley came in. He was carrying a suitcase. Bernard didn't quite know what to do, so he pretended he hadn't seen him.

"Hello, Bernard."

The concierge turned around and said nothing. Ian had lost a lot of weight and he wondered how he'd done it.

"How did your summer go?" asked Bernard, holding out his hand.

Ian shook it and gave him a broad smile.

Still smiling, Ian went through to reception, expecting Linda Orizio would be there. But there was nobody to be seen. Feeling disconcerted, he walked over to the Learning Room. As soon as he set his foot in the door...

"Surprise!" chorused the entire staff.

Ian greeted them all with tears in his eyes, saying he was sorry to each and every one of them. He gave an especially warm hug to Emmanuelle Evans and Alice Osaka, who'd brought little Luke along to the office. Any remaining resistance of Ian's melted when he saw the boy.

"I want to make an announcement: I'm going to be a father!" he said loudly and enthusiastically.

Some odd glances went around, so he went on, "My wife and I have decided to adopt a Madagascan child!"

Warm congratulations were given by all.

Then, Ian opened his briefcase and took out the list of ten points. It was framed in glass and wood. They all watched as he put it back in its rightful place. In the midst of all the commotion, George Lovejoy and Paul Prince appeared. Ian ran over to them and wordlessly hugged George with all his strength.

"Thank you so much, George."

"It was my pleasure, you philosopher, you!" joked the chairman, handing Ian back his letter.

Ian looked at Paul. The moment their eyes met, Ian couldn't hold back. He bowed his head and held out his hand in a reconciliatory gesture.

"I'm sorry Paul. Will you forgive me?"

Silence fell. All eyes were on Paul, who reached over and hugged Ian.

"There's nothing to forgive," he whispered inaudibly. "Welcome home."

The following day, Ian Insley was appointed general manager at SAT. Four years later, he was named Spanish director of the year. But ever since he's been back from Madagascar, his wife and child have become his two main priorities. Ian was never a religious man, but he does wear a pendant with one of the most often-quoted proverbs in Madagascar on it: "Izay rehetra ataonareo dia ataovy amin'ny fitiava," or, "Whatever you do, do it with love." He's never shown it to anyone in the firm, but he's sworn to practice it every day of his life.

EPILOGUE

**IF YOU REALLY WANT TO CHANGE THE WORLD,
START BY CHANGING YOURSELF.**

The best thing we can do for humankind is to learn to be at peace with ourselves. I admit it's taken me my whole life to learn what that means, but there's nothing I believe more strongly. Like most people, I also used to laugh at self-improvement books and personal growth seminars. I even used to aggressively demonize people who told me about mystical experiences of theirs involving intangible aspects of the human condition. I didn't know why at the time, but I found people like that really irritating.

How I've changed, though! I'm sixty-five years old, and the only thing I laugh at now is myself – my ignorance, my lack of awareness. You know what they say: 'None so blind as those who will not see.' Even now, it makes me shiver to think that. How could I have fooled myself for so many years? How could I have laughed at those who tried to show me the way? How could I have been so incredibly arrogant? How could I have been so out of touch with the only thing that keeps me alive? It's still a mystery to me.

But one thing I have discovered is that nothing happens by chance. Each one of us reaps what he sows. As Mahatma Gandhi, the great Indian leader, wrote, "Carefully watch your thoughts, for they become your words. Manage and watch your words, for they will become your actions. Consider and judge your actions, for they have become your habits. Acknowledge and watch your habits, for they shall become your values. Understand and embrace your values, for they become your destiny. And your destiny will become your life." A wise man, he was. I can't think of any better way of expressing the huge responsibility each of us has in managing his or her own life. Looking back and thinking about my own life, I realise that what has happened to me was generally not what I wanted or wished for, but what I needed in order to learn to be happy.

Life is so great when you become conscious, isn't it? It's such a great experience to be alive. Everything becomes so full of meaning when you follow your heart! I'm not a sentimental man, but I don't want to forget what really matters. I like to remind myself of it once in a while. Especially because the first fifty-seven years of my life went by almost without me realising. Luckily, life is so wise and generous it gave me the kiss of death. I'm talking seriously now: the triple bypass I had was an utter blessing. It opened my eyes. It was how I began to wake up and live. None of this would ever have happened if I hadn't gone through clinical death. Isn't it interesting, too, how I met Paul Prince just weeks afterwards. That's not his real name, as I said. It doesn't matter, though. What really matters is the imprint he left on all of us during the two and a half years he spent with us at SAT.

I still remember the first time I spoke to Paul. His meekness and integrity showed up my own fears and the gaps in my development. The revolution he caused in the company transformed all of us, including my dear friend Ian Insley, who today is an excellent general manager. Our scale of values changed radically, and on a personal level, I redefined what I meant by 'success'. With Paul, I learnt to bring what was most essential into the centre of my strategies, defining a new business mission: furthering the personal growth of our employees, developing and changing our own and our clients' organisational structure.

I'm quite certain now that when you trust in what you are not, you start to feel it in your heart. When you commit to what you feel, sooner or later it becomes real. Now, I trust fully that humankind, and the environment we live in, will become the centre of the new economic philosophy that the financial crisis will bring about. I'm not a visionary, I can't foresee the future; but I'm quite convinced that the only organisations that will survive are those which directly benefit humankind. All the rest will bring about their own failure.

The key to our future as a society is that each one of us commit, right now, to our own personal responsibility. It's no good playing the victim any more. Fear is the only thing that stops us from taking charge of our own lives. Unless we take responsibility for ourselves we're permanently condemned to being slaves to circumstance. But the more we grow and develop our inner selves, the more that truly productive, sustainable business projects will grow and evolve with the conscious evolution of humankind. I know it's hard to be brave. But that's why we're here, isn't it? To get over the fears that imprison us and become the people we can begin to be. It's all up to each one of us. And whether we care to admit it or not, it's a decision we make every day of our lives.

What we were and are, others will be. What we did and do will be done by others. It's 2010, and in spite of the crisis our consulting firm is growing and expanding.

The secret of our success is the fact that we're committed to serving others, to creating and generating real wealth for society. It's funny, too: now that I'm being invited to give talks, and sometimes come out in the newspapers, I realise that for me, true success means simply to feel peace and love in my heart. Thanks to that kind of fulfilment, I can be the caring husband my wife needs, and the loving father my three children want. What else could a happy human being ask for? Nothing. Nothing at all. Desire only appears when we feel empty and dissatisfied. Desire is such a dangerous thing! If we don't watch out it can carry us to the top of the world, but it will corrupt our souls.

Anyway, I'm sure you can imagine what happens when an old man like me is invited to share his thoughts with students at the big business schools or in respectable business circles. You should see how they stare at me! As if happiness were a forbidden word and being happy were a sin! But I don't pass judgement on them. How could I, when I perfectly understand them! I'd have stared, too, just a few years back. Their time will come, I'm sure. Changing and evolving human consciousness is necessary and unavoidable. It's just a matter of time before there's a shift in the way people think.

I'm back in touch with the playful, dreamy boy inside me. I know what I say is often greeted with scepticism and resistance, even though I focus on changing the individual mindset in order to change the way companies work – and by extension, to change the system. And so I'd encourage all those who are brave enough to hear me out to commit to learning about themselves and developing personally. Interestingly, when it's time for questions after I speak publicly, most adults only care about what I think about the crisis. But young people often ask me about Paul Prince. I can see he inspires them. Just before I finish off, I always say the same thing: 'I don't know exactly where he is now, or what he's doing. But I do know, if someone ever comes into your company saying he's the new Personal and Corporate Values Manager, get ready for a real revolution. And if he comes into your lives, do this for me: write to me straight away, and tell me that the Little Prince is back..."

THE CHAIRMAN
29th January 2010.

THANKS

Ever since my own mindshift took place, I've realised that life has always been really generous to me. When I look back, all I feel and want to express is gratitude. To my mother, I give thanks for having brought me into the world and having awoken my curiosity towards the secrets of the human soul. I want to thank my sister Linda, too, for her unconditional help and support for everything I do, and my brother Santiago for inspiring me with intelligence and ingenuity, and for accompanying me in my dreams and the things I search for. I also want to thank my friends, Pepe Barguñó, Víctor Gay Zaragoza, Javier Martínez de Marigorta, Marc Marín, Gregory Norris-Cervetto, Marc Oromí, Maria Orizio, Sebastián Skira y Gonzalo Vilar, for sharing my vision of consciousness as life's great alchemist. To my friend Clara Asmarats for her humility and bravery in being my first coachee. To Marta Sardà for taking me through a truly transformative coaching process. And to Irene Orce for being the most wonderful thing that's ever happened to me. With you I'm learning to LOVE, in capital letters. In publishing this book I'd also like to express my gratitude towards Alvar Canela, Víctor Cortadellas, Jorge Florit, Fernando Martorell, Daldo Murtra and Quique Teixedor: it was with all of you that I discovered my passion for story-telling. And Carlos Stampa, for encouraging me to enrol in Humanities and study Journalism. Thanks, too, to Antonio Morenés for asking me to send him regular emails and showing me my vocation as a writer. And to José Maria Piera and Luis Tusell for motivating me to try for the UAM-El País Master in Journalism. To my dad, for financing all my studies and giving me the freedom to become my own person. To Clara de Cominges for opening the way for my internship as a writer for *El País,* Barcelona. To Jesús Duva and Sebastián Tobarra for being the first bosses to trust me. To Serafí del Arco and Claudi Pérez, for helping me take my first steps as a financial journalist. To Tomás Delclós for taking me on as a writer for the Property supplement. To Amaya Iríbar for letting me write on business psychology and philosophy in the business. To Jesús Mota for having given me the chance to coordinate the Management and Training page. To Miguel Jiménez for his trust, companionship and unconditional support. To Goyo Rodríguez for his generosity in letting me into *El País Semanal.* To Sandra Bruna for trusting in our common literary project from the day it was conceived. To Jordi Nadal, for opening wide the doors to the publishing world for me. To Ana Lafuente, for believing in the message in this book and enriching it with her own passion and creativity. To the rest of the staff at Temas de Hoy publishers for making it possible for a manuscript to reach its readers as a book. And to Antoine de Saint-Exupéry, for having created such an unforgettable, inspiring character.

I'd like to thank the following friends and experts for their bravery and companionship:

Mario Alonso, Ignacio Álvarez de Mon, Santiago Álvarez de Mon,

Maite Barón, Maria Mercè Conangla, Juan Carlos Cubeiro, Nuria

Chinchilla, Andrea Gay, Xavier Guix, Manuel Giraudier, Herminia Gomà, Gerard Guiu, Pilar Jericó, Alicia Kaufmann, Fredy Kofman, Gonzalo Martínez de Miguel, Guillermo Martorell, Douglas McEncroe, José Luis Montes, Santiago Niño Becerra, Meritxell Obiols, François Pérez, Andrés Pérez Ortega, Lorenzo di Pietro, Iñaki Piñuel, Ernesto Poveda, Marta Romo, Alex Rovira, Isabel Salama, Jaume Sanllorente, Enrique Simó, Joaquín Tamames, Fernando Trías de Bes, Valentí Valls and Montse Ventosa. Thanks to all of you for sharing your enthusiasm and wisdom with me.

I'd also like to thank executives and businessmen and women Josep Burcet, Jorge Díez, Sergio Durany, Amadeu Guarch, Jacinto Guerrero, Toni Jové, Carlos Losada, Francisco Martín Frías, Gabriel Masfurroll, Joan Antoni Melé, Patricia Mir, Miquel Montes, Chisco Olascoaga, Ignacio Orce, Luis de Osuna, Ramón Poll, Diego Sánchez Pullido, Paco Sosa, Avelino Suárez, Santiago Vázquez and Silvia Vílchez, for embodying the values businesses need.

And I want to thank Gonzalo Bernardos for being the first one to dare to bring personal growth into the university, giving me the chance to set up the Masters in Personal Development and Leadership at the University of Barcelona. To all the students who have had the humility to allow me to do what I love the most: teaching.

And finally, I'd like to thank you, the reader, for being a part of the destiny of this book.

More information in www.borjavilaseca.com

Printed in Great Britain
by Amazon